TWO IN ONE FLESH

Part Three

THE PRACTICE OF SEX AND MARRIAGE

WITH ILLUSTRATIONS FROM THE CATHOLIC LITURGY

TWO IN ONE FLESH

PART ONE   An Introduction to Sex and Marriage.

PART TWO   The Mystery of Sex and Marriage in Catholic Theology.

PART THREE The Practice of Sex and Marriage.

From an Engraving
By
Eric Gill
Reproduced by kind permission of Mrs. Gill.

THE PRACTICE OF SEX AND MARRIAGE

WITH ILLUSTRATIONS FROM THE CATHOLIC LITURGY

by the
Rev. E. C. MESSENGER, Ph.D. (Louvain)

THE NEWMAN PRESS
Westminster, Maryland

Nihil Obstat: Thomas E. Bird, S.T.D., Ph.D.
Censor deputatus

Imprimatur: Joseph,
Archiepiscopus Birmingamiensis.
Birmingamiae, die 9a februarii 1948.

SANDS & CO. (PUBLISHERS) LTD.
15 KING STREET, COVENT GARDEN
LONDON, W.C. 2
76 CAMBRIDGE STREET
GLASGOW

MADE AND PRINTED IN GREAT BRITAIN BY
EBENEZER BAYLIS AND SON, LTD., THE
TRINITY PRESS, WORCESTER, AND LONDON

CONTENTS

CHAPTER   PAGE

I   INTRODUCTION   -   -   -   -   -   -   I

II   SEX ACCORDING TO SCIENCE   -   -   -   -   3

III   SEX, PSYCHOLOGY AND EDUCATION   -   -   -   -   8

IV   THE SOCIAL ASPECT OF SEX -   -   -   -   -   10

V   THE CHOICE OF A STATE IN LIFE -   -   -   -   16

VI   THE CHOICE OF A PARTNER -   -   -   -   -   18

VII   THE MARRIAGE CEREMONY AND ITS ACCOMPANIMENTS   21

VIII   THE SEX ACT AS AN EXPRESSION OF MUTUAL LOVE   -   27

IX   THE RELIGIOUS CHARACTER OF THE SEX ACT -   -   31

X   WHEN SHOULD SEXUAL INTERCOURSE TAKE PLACE?   34

XI   THE RELIGIOUS ASPECT OF PREGNANCY   -   -   40

XII   THE CHURCH AND CHILDBIRTH   -   -   -   -   44

XIII   THE SIZE OF THE FAMILY -   -   -   -   -   48

XIV   BIRTH CONTROL   -   -   -   -   -   -   52

XV   FAMILY LIFE AND PRAYERS -   -   -   -   -   58

XVI   THE SEX INSTRUCTION OF CHILDREN   -   -   -   61

        APPENDIX—SELECT BIBLIOGRAPHY -   -   -   -   66

"Live joyfully with the wife whom thou lovest, all the days of thy unsteady life, which are given to thee under the sun, all the time of thy vanity, for this is thy portion in life"

(*Eccles.* ix, 9).

"Husbands, love your wives, as Christ also loved the Church. . . . Even thus ought husbands to love their wives as their own bodies"

(*Ephesians* v., 25, 28, *Westminster Version*).

CHAPTER ONE

INTRODUCTION

In the preceding parts of this work,[1] we have set forth, first a certain narrow view of sex still alas! prevalent amongst some Catholics; next we have tried to show that the true Catholic teaching gives a much saner and indeed nobler view of sex in general, and of marriage in particular. We have shown, first the essential and natural character of sex from the standpoint of biological science, then its philosophical justification, and finally we have given a comprehensive survey of the teaching concerning sex in the sources of the Christian Revelation, i.e., Scripture and Tradition. In the course of our study, we have encountered some ideas which certainly tend to what has been called "sexual pessimism", and which doubtless account for the somewhat low view of sex which is still so prevalent to-day. But at the same time, our study has made it clear that the main stream of Christian Tradition has not really been favourable to these unsatisfactory and inadequate ideas. So far from sex being something evil in itself, or at most a concession wrung somewhat unwillingly from the Almighty because of original sin, the general Christian idea is that sex is something essentially holy in itself, and though doubtless affected more or less accidentally by human sin, it remains a divine institution, and substantially part of the divine plan. Furthermore, Christ our Lord has exalted sex to a new dignity by elevating marriage to the rank of a Christian Sacrament.

Side by side with this elevation of sex, we have found a definite assertion of the essential superiority of the virginal life—not indeed in itself, or for its own sake, but as a state adopted for higher religious motives. Moreover—and this is important—we have seen that this state of virginity is, in the view of some of the Church's greatest Fathers and theologians, praiseworthy only in the present fallen state of mankind. If man had not fallen, then the unmarried state would not have been praiseworthy. In a sense, virginity would have been present then, even in the married state, but it would have been a virginity compatible with married relations, and one which itself was fruitful, and would have resulted in parenthood. We have pointed out that similarly, the transcendent greatness and wonder of

---

[1] Part One: *Introduction to Sex and Marriage*; Part Two, *The Mystery of Sex and Marriage*.

Our Lady's Virginity arose precisely from the fact that it was a *fruitful* Virginity, making her to be a true Mother, first of her Divine Son, and then, in the spiritual order, of all Christians. And we have pointed out how, in the Church's conception, the virginity of those who choose the higher state must similarly be a fruitful one, resulting in spiritual parenthood.

Lastly, we have seen that, in some matters of detail, such as the lawfulness of the use of the sex act apart from the purpose of procreation, and the desirability of abstinence from sex on the part of married people from time to time, the views of the Church's theologians have undergone a certain measure of fluctuation and change, and that the stern views of earlier days in this regard are no longer favoured.

Having thus given a more or less historical account of the development of the Christian idea of sex, and an exposition of the Developed Theology of Sex, we now proceed to give a *practical* exposition of the whole subject, with special reference to married people, utilising the material found in Christian Tradition, and introducing some features of the Church's liturgy. We do so in the hope that this treatment will be found more satisfactory, and—dare we say it—more in the line of traditional Christian thought than the narrow and "low" view which we have throughout been combating. But it seems advisable first to advert once more to the scientific aspect of the matter, and this will enable us to show how the Christian idea, in the form in which we have outlined it, harmonises with scientific data, and how baseless are some modern non-Catholic views.

CHAPTER TWO

SEX ACCORDING TO SCIENCE

To begin with, then, the study of Natural History as developed by the biological sciences has shown us that all living things have the power to reproduce their kind, and that, in the higher organic beings, this is brought about by the union of two individuals of different sexes. The differentiation of sex organically considered obviously exists for the sake of reproduction. Every living being begins as a single cell, and in the higher organisms there are certain cells set aside for the purpose of reproduction, which are called gametes or germ cells. In species where the sexes differ, the special biological characteristic of the male and female gametes or germ cells is that, from the biological point of view, they are incomplete, inasmuch as they normally contain only half the number of chromosomes which are characteristic of the species in question. They may thus, in a sense, be called "half cells". The male and female gametes also differ in form. The female gametes are ovular in form, while the male gametes are longer and usually more mobile. Normally a female ovum cannot develop unless it is "fertilised" by union with a male gamete, though in some organisms such a development can be induced by various means. In any case, the normal thing is for a new individual of the species to result from the union of two gametes of different sex.

The female gametes are stored in the body of the female, in a receptacle called the ovary; the male gametes are formed in the testicles, and suitably stored. The male and female organs are essentially designed with a view to their mutual conjunction, when, by a marvellous mechanism, the male gametes are injected into the female genital canal, where one will probably meet a female ovum, and fertilise it by union, and immediately the wonderful process of embryonic growth begins. In the higher animals, this growth takes place inside the body of the female, and continues until the new individual is sufficiently organised and developed to exist as a separate being in the world, and this comes about by birth.

It seems obvious, then, that the differentiation of the sexes, and their union in the conjugal act, is biologically for the purpose of reproduction. The sex act essentially consists, from the physiological and biological standpoint, in the impelling of male gametes into the female genital canal, where they may meet a female ovum and fertilise it. If, then, from the standpoint of science, anything in the world has a purpose, the object, purpose, and *raison d'être* of sex is the reproduction of the species.

One would have thought it hardly necessary to stress this. But unfortunately, there are a number of non-Catholic writers on sex who have urged that reproduction is not in reality the purpose of sex from the biological point of view. This matter is so important that it deserves careful consideration. We will accordingly first set out this opposing view, and examine the grounds upon which it is based. Then we will briefly vindicate the traditional Catholic view which has aleady been set forth in detail in Part Two of this work.

What we may call the "non-generative" view of sex is set forth in various works. One presentation of it will be found in the section on Sex included in the *Outline of Modern Knowledge* published in 1931, and subsequently reprinted in separate form. It is written by no less an authority than Professor F. A. E. Crew, M.D., D.Sc., Ph.D., F.R.S.E., Professor of Animal Genetics and Director of the Animal Breeding Station in the University of Edinburgh.

He allows that "one is almost driven to the view that the nature and meaning of sex can only be recognised by bringing it into a definite and essential relation with reproduction" (p. 256). Science and its needs insist that "sex can only be understood and justified by postulating that it is the mechanism which Nature has ever used for the preservation of the species and for the improvement of the race" (p. 256). In addition "Morals . . . as taught by cleric and philosopher, unhesitatingly state that sex is the servant of reproduction". But "such views . . . are not contributions of the (biological) science itself, but impositions born of sociological necessity or of theological preference. They have a definitely degrading influence upon the logical structure of biology" (p. 257).

Next, Dr. Crew remarks that "the scientist of to-day does not concern himself with the meaning and the purpose of things": he leaves that to philosophy. He suggests that "the chief reason for the prevalence of" the "reproductive" point of view is "the impact of Jewish theology upon the sex-ethic of other peoples. Against it, he urges that "there have been peoples, such as the aborigines of Australia and the inhabitants of the South Sea Islands, who have been entirely unaware of the connection between sexual intercourse and reproduction."[1] Dr. Crew adds that "to other peoples, the Greeks for example, sex has been justified simply and completely by

---

[1] The facts are by no means so certain as Dr. Crew seems to think. He should read G. E. Newsom's *New Morality* on the supposed ignorance of sex and consequent promiscuity of the Trobriand islanders. See also Part Two of the present work, p. 166.

sexual desire." Thus, the "reproductive" point of view "has not been universally accepted". Furthermore, "when the matter is considered dispassionately, it will be found that it is impossible to endorse it by an honest appeal to scientific fact. It is true that sexual activity commonly precedes, leads up to, and passes on to reproductive activity". But "reproduction leads to sexuality just as much as sexuality leads to reproduction".

Then Dr. Crew goes a step further, and speaks of "the possible separation of sex and reproduction". Asexual reproduction is "as widespread as is reproduction with mating. Manifestly, therefore, sexuality is not essential for reproduction" (p. 259). It is "not the only means of reproduction" (p. 260). Moreover, "sexuality does not seem to possess any real advantage over asexuality in the matter of reproduction" (p. 264).

Again, "the personal value of the sexual act is not necessarily reduced after sterilisation. . . . Sexual activity without reproductive activity is as possible as reproduction without sex. . . . The pleasure of sexual activity has no relation to reproduction. It is present whether coitus is fruitful or abortive". And there, apparently, Dr. Crew is prepared to leave the matter. He concludes with an expression of "regret that biologists and laymen could not be content to leave the nature of sex unexplained".

Here are some quotations, from other writers. The Rev. Dr. Weatherhead, in his *Mastery of Sex*, published by the Student Christian Movement, rejects "the view that intercourse should never take place unless a child is desired" (pp. 80, 184), and quotes a lady missionary in China who says that "the false idea that intercourse undertaken for a reproductive purpose is more meritorious than intercourse performed purely as an expression of love, is dying: it never had any foundation in reason or science" (p. 239).

Similarly, Dr. David Mace, in his *Does Sex Morality Matter?* asserts that "sexual intimacy is right and good in itself, as an expression of affection", apart from its creative purpose. "It has, as a matter of fact, a good many other consequences than the production of children". Accordingly, he advocates conception control, but refers the reader to a doctor in the matter of choice of a method. Similar advice is given by the Rev. Dr. Weatherhead in the book[1]

[1] The Rev. L. Weatherhead's actual words are: "Women should not be put off by doctors who discourage them" (from using birth control devices) "from other than medical reasons. Nor is it to be supposed that most general practitioners know much about the subject. . . . Further, many doctors, acting merely from prejudice, dissuade married people from practising birth control when there is no real basis for such dissuasion. However, doctors are now fortunately to be found who know their subject and who can and will do all that is required" (!). (*The Mastery of Sex*, 1946 edn., p. 79). The book is published by the Student Christian Movement, and by 1946 had reached fifteen editions, making 76,000 copies!

already mentioned. He seems to go out of his way to advocate
birth control, and even tells his readers that they should disregard
the opinion of their family doctor if he is opposed to the practice!

In the work already mentioned, Dr. David Mace quite logically
refuses to say that "the union of true lovers apart from marriage is
impure": it is only "a very serious mistake" (p. 61). In an Appendix
to his work, contributed by Dr. A. Charles E. Gray, M.D., we read:

> "It is argued by some that the sexual act should be restricted
> to occasions when there is a definite intention of begetting child-
> ren. This does not seem either reasonable or desirable. Nature's
> plans were certainly, in the case of human beings, not constructed
> on that basis. . . . As Havelock Ellis has put it: 'Even if sexual
> relationships had no connection with procreation whatever, they
> would still be justifiable. . . .' Sexual intimacy has a value in itself
> as an expression in the terms of the body which unites husband
> and wife" (p. 199).

In some works, we find an argument based upon the prodigality
of nature in the matter of coitus. It is urged that reproduction cannot
be the real or sole purpose of the sexual act, seeing that in every
human union, the male emits some two million spermatozoa, only
one of which could normally fertilise a female ovum. Similarly
it is urged that there are very many female ova which are doomed
never to be fertilised. And finally, there are many sex unions which
are unfruitful from purely natural causes.

As to the first form of the argument, surely this betrays very
shallow thinking. The prodigality of nature in the sex union is
rather an argument for the "reproductive" interpretation of the
sex act. Nature is evidently so bent upon producing the desired
result, i.e., the perpetuation of the species, that she produces an
enormous number of gametes, precisely to ensure the result in spite
of possible failures.

The other arguments are just as fallacious. The unfruitfulness of
some sex unions, when not deliberate, is the effect of some physiological defect. As to the supposed ignorance of the natural outcome
of the sex act in certain tribes, this is surely no proof that the natural
result and purpose of the act is not reproduction. There is an
obvious confusion here between things which were clearly dis-
tinguished as long ago as the thirteenth century, the *finis operis* and
the *finis operantis*. We have explained this in a chapter in Part Two.
Even a superficial examination of sex differentiation and the union
of the two sexes in the act of coitus serves to show that the sex act
is naturally and essentially destined to bring about the union of the

germ cells or gametes, with the resulting production of offspring.

As to the argument that the sex act has other results and characteristics, especially in man, we do not deny the existence of these. In fact, we shall discuss some of them in the course of this Part Three. But it remains true that, biologically, the primary purpose of sex is the reproduction of the species.

The union of the sexes, then, is natural and normal. And inasmuch as it is destined and intended primarily for the continuation of the species, and this requires in the case of the human race a permanent association between man and woman, marriage, precisely as this permanent association, is natural to man. And precisely because it is natural to man, it is, in the Church's view, a divine institution. Further, inasmuch as the sex act is intended primarily for the production of children, its exercise is lawful only in the permanent association of man and woman which we call marriage. And in that union it must always be exercised with that primary end in view, or at least this primary end must never be positively and deliberately excluded, or prevented.

CHAPTER THREE

SEX, PSYCHOLOGY AND EDUCATION

So far we have dealt only with the physiological aspect of sex, i.e., the existence of different sex organs and their use. But it is most important for all to bear in mind the existence of what are called "secondary" sex characteristics, of a physiological nature, and furthermore, of important differences in the mental constitution and outlook of male and female. Sex and sexual differentiation play a far larger part in our lives than many of us are aware. The reason is that sexual differentiation and development affect the whole organism in varying degrees, and have their counterpart also in mental development. This is very obvious in the case of the female. From the physiological point of view, as soon as the age of puberty is reached we get the phenomenon known as menstruation, which is so obviously connected with sex life.[1] When a woman has her *menses*, she often feels uncomfortable physically, and suffers from a corresponding moodiness mentally. Again, a woman, even from early girlhood, is attracted by dolls, and still more by real babies—an indication that her whole constitution and mental outlook is precisely that of a woman.

Though they are not so obvious, there are similar sexual characteristics in the outlook of every man and boy. The development of the sex organs at puberty will often be accompanied by a certain mental instability, an attitude of reserve in presence of the other sex, and a general change in mental outlook, the meaning of which will not be clearly understood at the time. Childhood, in which the sexes are *comparatively* undifferentiated mentally—but only comparatively—is giving place to manhood and womanhood, in which the sexes are markedly distinct in every way. The male characteristics of sex are developing fast, and are beginning to make themselves felt in new ways. Small wonder that the mental outlook of a boy at this stage is not altogether a stable one. It may even manifest itself in religious as well as moral difficulties, but a wise parent or counsellor will not be dismayed, but will realise that this is only a

---

[1] Menstruation consists in the ejection of an unfertilised ovum, together with the various tissues and substances which Nature has already prepared in anticipation of fertilisation and conception.

passing phase, which needs patience and sympathy rather than condemnation or criticism.

We may sum all this up by saying that, from the natural standpoint, every boy and man is a potential husband and father, and every girl and woman is a potential wife and mother.

Another important truth is the fact that the two sexes are not really antagonistic to each other, but are intended by nature to be complementary to each other. The fully developed male has characteristics both physical and mental which are quite definitely manly. Equally, the fully developed female has characteristics which are womanly. And each sex is intended by Nature to find its full complement in the society of the other. Man was made for woman, and woman similarly was made for man. Man naturally desires the society and companionship of woman, and woman equally desires the society and companionship of man. The two sexes were intended by God to supplement each other, and to find their full development in their union in the married state.

This essential differentiation, both physical and mental, between male and female cannot be destroyed by human efforts, though much may be done in an attempt to obliterate it. The results of such attempts are by no means worthy of admiration. Who can admire a weak and womanly man? And who can admire a woman who apes masculine ways?

The differentiation between male and female should be respected by all, and especially in the matter of the education of children, both physical and mental. Hence the Church is rightly opposed, as a rule, to "co-education", in which the same treatment is meted out to boys and girls in all stages of their school lives. Rather, the type of education given to a boy should be precisely that which will fit him to be a husband and a father, and his sports and games should be chosen accordingly. And on the other hand, a girl should be educated precisely to be a woman, who will normally become a wife and a mother. There is no need to amplify this educational truism here.

This distinction in education and training will involve a certain measure of separation, and perhaps even of segregation, for a time. But care should be taken not to allow such segregation to take any extreme form, or to result in any depreciation of the opposite sex as an unnecessary or undesirable part of God's creation. Rather, care should be taken throughout to emphasise that God's plan requires the existence of both sexes, and that these two sexes are intended by God normally to live together in harmonious union in the marriage state.

CHAPTER FOUR

THE SOCIAL ASPECT OF SEX

THE fact that the two sexes are complementary, as we have said, resulting as it does in each having its allotted sphere in life, should obviate any tendency to emphasise the superiority of one sex over the over, and prevent any rivalry between them. A man's destiny is normally to work to support himself, his wife and his family. A woman's destiny is to be the wife of a man, and the mother of his children. In other words, her natural and normal place is to reign in a home as its mistress. In any group or society of human beings there must, of course, be some kind of head, and in the human family, the Church, following the dictates both of Nature and Revelation, insists that the headship belongs to the man. But equally the Church insists that there is to be no despotism in the family: the wife is a helpmate, not a slave or a chattel, and if the husband is the head, the wife may well be called the heart of the family. Man is guided predominantly by reason, woman, perhaps, predominantly by instinct and sentiment. Each requires the other. In practical life, as distinct from the theoretical sciences such as mathematics, few matters can be determined or dealt with satisfactorily by pure reason. Equally, pure instinct needs guidance and control, such as can be provided only by reason. The harmonious combination of reason and instinct can come about only by the careful adjustment and modification of one by the other, through the joint contribution by husband and wife in matters of family life. Thus do we find realised in practice the statement which Holy Scripture attributes to man's Creator: "it is not good for man to be alone; let us make him a help like unto himself" (*Genesis* ii, 18).

But, while the society and companionship of the opposite sex is a great help to each, it must be borne in mind that this mutual help is mainly, though not exclusively, with a view to the reproduction of the species. Indeed, as we have seen, St. Augustine went so far as to assert that he did not see how otherwise woman could be of help to man, if not to bear his children, for in other matters a man can be helped better by his own sex.[1] St. Thomas adopted the same opinion.[2]

[1] See Part One, p. 25.
[2] See Part One, pp. 25–26.

The help and companionship of the two sexes, then, is primarily with a view to the continuation of the species. This leads us to an important truth: the sex urge is concerned with man, not so much as an individual being, but rather as a member of the human species. In other words, sex, though an individual instinct, is primarily social in its implications. From this truth, again, many other important consequences follow. For instance, it is this social character of sex, especially when it results in the matrimonial association, that justifies the interest of the State in the civil aspect of the marriage contract and its effects—an interest which is fully recognised by the Church, even in Christian marriage, where the contract is elevated to the rank of a sacrament.

Of even greater importance is the truth that, as marriage is a social institution, and the sex urge is primarily social in its purpose, not all human beings are called upon to fulfil this social task of perpetuating the species. It is, of course, a well known fact that in certain species, and particularly in bees, there are individuals specially destined for the procreation of new individuals, whilst others are destined for different tasks in the life of the hive. These latter are sexually "neuters". There is, of course, nothing quite like this in man. Every normal human being is endowed with sexual organs and capabilities. Even so, there are some isolated individuals in whom the sex mechanism seems to have gone astray, and whose sex is either undeveloped, or difficult to determine. Moreover, as Mr. Kenneth Walker has written, "the strength of sexuality varies as much in different individuals as does the capacity to enjoy music. For some men and women, sexuality and all that it implies holds little interest; at no time in their lives have they given it more than a passing thought."[1] He adds that "these differences in the strength of the drive bear no relation to physique". Further on in the same work, he writes: "Continence of itself can do no bodily harm, and it may be that the athlete who, for the sake of the race he is about to run, abjures sexual activity, will find that he has enhanced rather than diminished his physical efficiency. . . . There are men whose sexual urge is so weak, or whose sublimation of it is so complete, that continence imposes upon them little if any hardship." Others, on the contrary, find the strain very great indeed. People also differ in "the efficiency of their means of combating" sexual desire. "If a man has conceived a certain ideal after which he strives, and for the sake of which he is willing to make any sacrifice, the path he follows is clearly marked. Whatever may be the hardships, he is prepared to face them with singleness of purpose." The task may be difficult, but, "hard as is the lot of a highly sexed man who sacrifices his

[1] *Physiology of Sex*, Pelican Books, p. 61.

sexual life for the sake of a positive ideal, it is incomparably easier
than that of a man who sacrifices it without having any religious
ideals."[1]

These two facts, namely, the truth that the sexual urge is primarily
social in its implication, and the consequent fact that not every
human individual feels an irresistible impulse to satisfy it physically,
provides the natural basis for the possibility of the supernatural
virtue of virginity, undertaken for God's sake, and for religious
motives. For we must repeat that, while celibacy may be chosen as
a matter of course by those who feel no special sex urge, it is not a
virtue unless it is chosen for religious motives, i.e., for the love of
God, and also, we will add, for the love of other human beings.
True Christian virginity, as we have insisted, is essentially social
in its outlook, as is marriage.

This will be the proper place to examine St. Thomas Aquinas's
justification of virginity. It will be found in two places in the *Summa
Theologica*: in IIa IIae, q. 152, art. 2, and in III Suppl., q. 41, art. 2.
In the former article, he is discussing "Whether Virginity is Unlawful", and he answers thus:

"In human acts, that is vicious which is outside right reason.
Now, right reason lays it down that one should use those things
which are means to an end according to the measure which corresponds to the end. But there are three human goods: one which
consists in external things such as riches, another which consists
in bodily goods, and a third which consists in goods of the soul,
amongst which the good things of a contemplative life are better
than those of an active life, as the Philosopher shows, and as Our
Lord says: 'Mary hath chosen the better part.' Among the external goods, there are some which are related to things of the
body, and those of the body are ordered to those of the soul, and
further, those of the active life are ordered to those of the contemplative life. Hence it belongs to right reason to use external
goods according to the measure which belongs to the body, and
similarly with the others. Hence, if one abstains from possessing
certain things which it would otherwise be good to possess, in
order to promote bodily health, or even the contemplation of
truth, this would not be vicious, but in accordance with right
reason. Similarly, if one abstains from bodily delights, in order
the more freely to give oneself to the contemplation of truth, this
is in accordance with right reason. Now, religious virginity[2]
abstains from all venereal pleasure precisely that it may make

---

[1] *Op. cit.*, pp. 73-74.
[2] Note the adjective: "*pia* virginitas".

divine contemplation easier, for the Apostle says: 'The unmarried woman and the virgin thinketh on the things of the Lord, that she may be holy both in body and in spirit: but she that is married thinketh on the things of the world, how she may please her husband.' Hence virginity is not something vicious, but rather praiseworthy.'[1]

So much for the general justification of religious virginity. The first Difficulty, however, urges that virginity is contrary to a precept of the law of nature. For just as there is a precept of this law aiming at the conservation of the individual, commanding us to eat, so there is also another precept ordering the conservation of the species, set forth in the words: "Increase and multiply, and fill the earth." Hence, just as it would be sinful to abstain from all food, so also it is sinful to abstain from all acts of generation.

St. Thomas answers this pertinent objection thus:

"A precept has the nature of a duty. Now, a duty may bind in two ways: first, it may need to be fulfilled by an individual, and this duty cannot be neglected without sin. But there may be another duty, which has to be fulfilled by the multitude, for many things are necessary for the multitude or community, which one individual does not suffice to fulfil, but which can be fulfilled by the multitude, in that one individual does this and another does that. The precept of the law of nature concerning eating has to be carried out by each individual, for otherwise the individual could not be conserved. But the precept concerning generation applies to the whole multitude of mankind. Now, it is necessary to the multitude not only that it should be multiplied bodily, but also that it should progress spiritually. And hence the multitude will

[1] "In humanis actibus, illud est vitiosum quod est praeter rectam rationem. Habet autem hoc recta ratio, ut his quae sunt ad finem utatur aliquis secundum eam mensuram quae congruit fini. Est autem triplex hominis bonum. . . .: unum quidem quod consistit in exterioribus rebus, puta divitiis; aliud autem quod consistit in bonis corporis; tertium autem quod consistit in bonis animae: inter quae etiam bona contemplativae vitae sunt potiora bonis vitae activae, ut Philosophus probat, et Dominus dicit: 'Maria optimam partem elegit.' Quorum bonorum exteriora quidem ordinantur ad ea quae sunt corporis; ea vero quae sunt corporis, ad ea quae sunt animae; et ulterius ea quae sunt vitae activae, ad ea quae sunt vitae contemplativae. Pertinet igitur ad rectitudinem rationis ut aliquis utatur exterioribus bonis secundum eam mensuram quae competit corpori: et similiter de aliis. Unde si quis abstineat ab aliquibus possidendis quae alias esset bonum possidere, ut consulat saluti corporali, vel etiam contemplationi veritatis, non esset hoc vitiosum, sed secundum rationem rectam. Et similiter si qui abstinet a delectationibus corporalibus, ut liberius vacet contemplationi veritatis pertinet hoc ad rectitudinem rationis. Ad hoc autem pia virginitas ab omni delectatione venerea abstinet, ut liberius divinae contemplationi vacet; dicit enim Apostolus: 'Mulier innupta et virgo cogitat quae Domini sunt, ut sit sancta et corpore et spiritu: quae autem nupta est, cogitat quae mundi sunt, et quomodo placeat viro.' Unde relinquitur quod virginitas non est aliquid vitiosum, sed potius laudabile."

be provided for sufficiently if some give themselves to the work of carnal generation, and others, abstaining from this, give themselves to the contemplation of divine things, for the glory and well being of the whole human race: just as in an army, some guard the camp, some carry the flag, and some fight with weapons; all these things being required by the multitude, but they cannot be fulfilled by one person."[1]

This well brings out the social advantages of virginity. For, just as those who give themselves to the duty of procreation are seeing to the welfare of the state from the material point of view, so also those who give themselves up to contemplation and the religious life are seeing to the welfare of the same State from the spiritual point of view.

Here is the other treatment of the same question, taken from St. Thomas's *Commentary on the Sentences,* and reprinted in the Supplement to the Third Part of the *Summa Theologica,* q. 41, art. 2:

"Nature can incline to a thing in two ways: in one way as to something necessary for the perfection of the individual, and this inclination is binding upon each and all. In another way, nature inclines to something which is necessary for the perfection of the multitude, and as there are many such things, some of which impede others, not every man is bound by such an inclination as by a precept; for otherwise every man would be bound to take up agriculture, and building, and other offices necessary for the life of the human community. But this natural inclination is satisfied if and when the various needs mentioned are satisfied by different individuals. Now, inasmuch as, for the perfection of the human community, it is necessary that some should devote themselves to the contemplative life, which is particularly hindered by matrimony, the natural inclination towards matrimony does not bind (every individual) after the manner of a precept."

[1] "Praeceptum habet rationem debiti. . . . Dupliciter autem aliquid est debitum: uno modo ut impleatur ab uno, et hoc debitum sine peccato praeteriri non potest; aliud autem est debitum implendum a multitudine; et ad tale debitum implendum non tenetur quilibet de multitudine; multa enim sunt multitudini necessaria, ad quae implenda unus non sufficit; sed implentur a multitudine, dum unus hoc, alius illud facit. Praeceptum igitur legis naturae homini datum de comestione, necesse est quod ab unoquoque impleatur: aliter enim individuum conservari non posset. Sed praeceptum datum de generatione respicit totam multitudinem hominum, cui necessarium est non solum quod multiplicetur corporaliter, sed etiam quod spiritualiter proficiat. Et ideo sufficienter providetur humanae multitudini, si quidam carnali generationi operam dent, quidam vero ab hac abstinentes, contemplationi divinorum vacent ad totius humani generis pulchritudinem et salutem; sicut etiam in exercitu quidam castra custodiunt, quidam signa deferunt, quidam gladiis decertant; quae tamen omnia debita sunt multitudini, sed per unum impleri non possunt."

We have inserted the words "every individual" here because it is obviously required by the sense. Elsewhere, i.e., in *Summa Theologica*, Ia IIae, q. 94, art. 2, St. Thomas asserts that there is an order of natural precepts corresponding to the order of natural inclinations in man. First there is in man a natural inclination which he shares with all beings, namely, the inclination to self preservation, and this has its counterpart in the natural law. Secondly, man shares one inclination with other animals, and this explains the existence of the natural law concerning the "union of male and female, and the bringing up of children". So St. Thomas admits that there are precepts concerning marriage and procreation. But he denies that the precept to marry and have children is binding upon each and every individual. Evidently it is binding on the race as such, and must be fulfilled by some individuals, for the sake of the community, while others, also for the sake of the community, choose a celibate life. Thus once more St. Thomas emphasises the social value of religious celibacy and virginity.

It may be wondered how this commendation of virginity as a blessing for the community as a whole can be reconciled with St. Thomas's clear statement, mentioned in Part Two of this work,[1] that virginity would *not* have been laudable in the state of innocence. We must refer the reader to our remarks on those previous pages, and also to the further discussion of the matter in Appendix One to Part Two.

While St. Thomas thus emphasises the social value of virginity, he is always careful to explain that, in the concrete, it is not meant for all human beings. Thus, in the *Summa Theologica*, Ia IIae, q. 108, art. 4, ad. 1, he explains that while the evangelical counsels may be said to be expedient for all, *in themselves*, they are not so in actual fact, because of the indisposition of some in their regard, for their leanings are not in this direction. He adds that for this reason, when Our Lord set forth the evangelical counsels, he always mentioned that they were for those fitted for them, and not for others.[2]

---

[1] See Part Two, pp. 22, 23, 25.

[2] "Praedicta consilia, quantum est de se, sunt omnibus expedientia, sed ex indispositione aliquorum contingit quod alicui expedientia non sunt, quia eorum affectus ad haec non inclinatur. Et ideo Dominus consilia evangelica proponens, semper facit mentionem de idoneitate hominum ad observantiam consiliorum. Dans enim consilium perpetuae paupertatis praemittit: 'Si vis perfectus esse,' et postea subdit: 'Vade, et vende omnia quae habes'. Similiter dans consilium perpetuae castitatis, cum dixit: 'Sunt eunuchi qui castraverunt seipsos propter regnum coelorum,' statim subdit: 'Qui potest capere capiat'. Et similiter Apostolus, praemisso consilio virginitatis, dicit: 'Porro hoc ad utilitatem vestram dico, non ut laqueum vobis injiciam.' "

CHAPTER FIVE

THE CHOICE OF A STATE IN LIFE

THE considerations set forth in the previous chapter must be given anxious and lengthy attention by each and every individual when he or she is determining his or her own state of life in the future. Some Christian thinkers in the past have tended, perhaps, to urge too freely the adoption of the celibate state, adding even that if the world should come to an end through all choosing virginity, this would be a most glorious consummation.[1] Others, taking a more sober and, in our opinion, a wiser view, have urged that the duty to increase and multiply must continue to be incumbent upon mankind until the number of God's elect has been filled up. And certainly we have no means of knowing when that will be, still less of asserting that the number is now complete. Hence it would seem presumptuous to urge all to embrace a celibate life, especially in view of the institution of the sacrament of matrimony for all time, and Our Lord's own intimation that celibacy is not for all, but only for those to whom it is given (*Matt*. xix, 11).[2]

Those who, after prayer and due consideration, and consultation with others, think that they are indeed called to a single life, should then ask themselves whether this call cannot be better obeyed by entering the ranks of the priesthood, or the religious life. There they will find all the helps which the age-long experience of the Church has suggested, to keep untarnished their high ideal, and to retain both the religious and the social character of their sacrifice.

We can here profitably discuss the question of the right of all to marry. The Church is certainly opposed absolutely to any denial of the rights of ordinary human beings to marry, and Pope Pius XI made this perfectly clear in his *Encyclical on Christian Marriage*. In this he especially condemns those eugenists who "would have the public authority forbid marriage to any persons who, in the light of the laws and conjectures of eugenic science, are deemed likely through heredity to beget defective offspring, even though they may be in all essential respects fit to marry."

But though the Pope thus vindicates the right of all to marry, he does not say that this right should always be exercised and in all

[1] Cf. Part One, p. 11.
[2] Cf. Part Two, p. 118.

cases. Indeed, he remarks that "it is often well to dissuade" those who will only beget defective offspring, from entering the married state. This should be taken in conjunction with the Pope's statement that those who contemplate marriage should bear in mind that it is a social institution, and the fountain-head of civil society. There may well be cases in which, because of some serious physical or mental defect which is likely to be transmitted to any offspring, a well-disposed and religious person will abstain from exercising his or her right to marry. The late Père Fallon, S.J., wrote as follows: "No one may, for the sake of his personal interest or for the satis-faction of a personal sentiment, impose a charge upon others or create a peril for them. . . . Those who, in bringing children into the world, would have the certain prospect of making them a charge upon institutions of hospitalisation, or of creating for others a new source of contagion or of grave disorders, with no likelihood of compensation or remedy, would be morally bound in principle, and apart from exceptional circumstances, to abstain from marriage."[1] That was written before the appearance of Pope Pius XI's *Encyclical on Marriage*, and doubtless many Catholics would not care now to go so far. In place of being "morally bound to abstain from marriage", it might be better to describe the persons in question as to be "dissuaded" from entering into matrimony, to use the Pope's own term, adding with the Pope that "those who on other counts are capable of marriage, even though, granted every care and attention, it is surmised that they will only beget defective offspring, are certainly not to be accused of a serious crime if they enter the married state."[2]

Economic considerations should doubtless be given due weight by those who propose to marry, and no man should enter this state unless and until he is capable of supporting a wife and family. The application of this principle to the idea expressed in the phrase "Love on the Dole" may be left to the reader. Certainly, no self-respecting man would ask a woman he really loved to live a life of destitution or degradation, or to bring into the world new human beings who would be compelled to share such conditions. The Christian virtues of prudence and temperance would surely dictate otherwise, as well as the virtue of charity.

[1] *Eugenics*, p. 45.
[2] C.T.S. edition, p. 31.

CHAPTER SIX

THE CHOICE OF A PARTNER

HAVING dealt with the favoured few called to serve God in the priesthood or in religion, and with those unfortunates who renounce their right to marry for other adequate reasons, we now pass on to the many, whose call it is undoubtedly to serve God and humanity in the married state. Their early training and education will, it is hoped, have kept this ultimate destiny well in view. And wise parents, educators and others will have provided ample and suitable opportunities for the meeting and mixing of the sexes, so that each may have every chance of selecting a suitable life partner.

Pope Pius XI wrote some very wise words in this connection, which deserve to be quoted:

> "Of the first importance in the proximate preparation for matrimony is the careful choice of a partner. On this, indeed, depends for the most part the happiness or unhappiness of marriage, because each partner may be to the other either a great help or else a great danger and hindrance in the leading of a Christian married life. An imprudent choice may be the source of a lifetime of regrets, and therefore those about to marry ought to reflect carefully before choosing the person with whom they will have to spend the remainder of their lives. In this reflection they should give the first place to the consideration of God and the true religion of Christ; then they should consider themselves, their future offspring, and also the human race and the nation, of which matrimony is the source."[1]

Note here how the Pope urges people to remember the social character of matrimony in the choice of a partner. The Pope continues:

> "Let them fervently ask God's help to make their choice with Christian prudence; not under the influence of an unreasoning and unbridled passion; not out of the sole desire of monetary gain or any other less noble motive; but guided by a true and upright love and sincere affection towards their partner, and seeking in marriage the ends for which God instituted it."[2]

[1] C.T.S. edn., p. 54.
[2] *Ibid.*

Note here that the Pope condemns loveless marriages which are simply "arranged" for temporal reasons. Marriages should be based on a "true and upright love and sincere affection". His Holiness concludes:

> "Let them not forget, finally, to ask the prudent advice of their parents. To this advice they should attach great value, since their maturer judgment and experience may save them from making a disastrous mistake in this matter. They will thus enter upon the sacred state of matrimony hallowed abundantly with the blessing of the fourth commandment: 'Honour thy father and mother. . . .' "[1]

Many unhappy marriages would be avoided if more care were exercised in entering this holy state. In the presence of so many marriages which are manifest failures, modern writers often proceed to condemn the institution of marriage itself, or at least to urge that there should be ample facilities for divorce, or even for "trial marriages". But surely, the failures are not due to the institution itself, or to the indissolubility of the contract, but to the folly and thoughtlessness, and sometimes irrational and almost criminal haste with which some people enter upon this sacred state. Due care should be taken to obtain full knowledge of the other's character, disposition and circumstances, physical and mental. In at least one Catholic country it is the custom for the parties proposing to marry to exchange information on the medical history of the families, and for this there can be nothing but praise. In this respect we can agree with the sensible remarks of Mr. Kenneth Walker in his *Physiology of Sex*:

> "The majority of modern writers on the subject of marriage are in favour of a full medical examination of both parties before the proposed marriage is announced. At this examination, all questions relating to the marital relationship and parenthood are freely discussed. It has even been argued by some enthusiasts that the production of a certificate of medical fitness should be made compulsory before any wedding is solemnized. In spite of the advantages that would result from this, such as the discovery that one of the parties was marrying while still suffering from communicable venereal disease, it would be difficult in a democratic country, where personal liberty is so jealously guarded, to make it compulsory. Our efforts can at any rate be directed to

[1] *Ibid.*

rendering it customary whenever any doubts exist as to the health of either party."[1]

A partner should thus be chosen after much deliberation, careful thought and inquiry. Every effort should be made to get to know the other person thoroughly, in all aspects, and especially in his or her home life. A shrewd observer will be able to tell what sort of life-partner a young man or young woman will make, from the way he or she behaves in the home towards other members of the family. Parents should do all in their power to keep "open house" for the friends of their children, and this will also enable themselves to form a judgment upon the character of those with whom their children are associating.

Once a choice is made, there will sooner or later be a formal engagement. The Church's Canon Law provides for a public or solemn engagement or promise of future marriage, expressed in writing and signed by the two parties and by the bishop or parish priest, or at least by two other witnesses. Unfortunately, such engagements are no longer the custom in our own country. Perhaps it would be better if they were. In any case, we have our own custom of announcing an engagement, and the giving of an engagement ring to the lady chosen.

The question of a long or a short engagement depends upon many circumstances, and need not be dealt with here. But one word must be said of the difficulties attached to this state. The two parties must be presumed to be in love with each other—for other-wise an engagement would be a mockery. Quite naturally, this love will seek expression. But equally, it is clear that any sexual union or intercourse is morally wrong under the circumstances for, as we have seen, this is essentially destined for the procreation of children in the married state. Hence any expression of affection which arouses sexual feelings or desires must be avoided. This will, of course, be difficult. But the best way is to have a clear idea of the nature and function of sex desire, and to bear in mind always that true love is, not getting, but giving. That is the difference between sensual lust and true human love. Sensual desire wants its own satisfaction; true love manifests itself in the desire to give oneself wholly to one's partner, for his or her sake. The sensual satisfaction which accom-panies this surrender and sacrifice of self is the divinely ordained reward, but should not be the direct and immediate object aimed at. This consideration, if borne in mind, may help to repel unworthy and untimely desires. Prayer and the Sacraments will bring super-natural help in this regard.

[1] p. 106.

CHAPTER SEVEN

THE MARRIAGE CEREMONY AND ITS ACCOMPANIMENTS

At length the happy day dawns, and the marriage takes place. We assume throughout that it will be a truly Catholic wedding, and that both parties will be united and in agreement on the most solemn matters of time and eternity. How otherwise could there be complete domestic harmony and happiness?

A Catholic marriage will naturally be a full and complete one, beginning with the wedding itself, and then proceeding to the Nuptial Mass.

The wedding rite itself has a beautiful prayer for the blessing of the ring:

> "Bless, O Lord, this ring, which we bless in thy name, that she who shall wear it, keeping true faith unto her husband, may abide in thy peace and according to thy will, and ever live in love given and taken. Through Christ our Lord. Amen."

The ring will henceforth be a very precious possession of the wife, and a sign and symbol also to the husband of the treasure which God has entrusted to his keeping and protection.

Here it is of interest to recall that in 1935 the late Cardinal Hinsley, Archbishop of Westminster, petitioned the Holy See to grant a partial indulgence of ten days, to be gained once a day by husband and/or wife who, at least with a contrite heart, should kiss the wedding ring, and utter a certain ejaculatory prayer, or a similar one. The prayer suggested was the following:

> "Grant us, O Lord, that loving Thee, we may love each other, and live according to Thy Holy Law."

This petition was favourably received by the Holy See, and the indulgence desired was granted, in favour of the faithful of the Archdiocese of Westminster, for seven years from July 13th, 1935. Ten years later, i.e., on July 5th, 1945, the Sacred Penitentiary in Rome issued a Rescript extending the indulgence for a further seven years from that date, for the faithful of the Archdiocese of Westminster only. It is to be hoped that the grant of this indulgence

will some day be made permanent, and extending to the other
dioceses of this country.

We pass on now to the Nuptial Mass. Too often Catholics fail
to avail themselves of this supreme and glorious privilege of kneel-
ing together before God's altar while the Holy Sacrifice is offered
specially for their intentions, and to bring down God's blessing
upon their new life. Yet not only is there a special Mass for this
occasion, with its own Introit, Collect, Epistle, Gradual, Gospel,
Offertory, Communion and Post-Communion,[1] but in addition,
immediately after the *Pater Noster*, the celebrant interrupts the
normal sequence of the Mass and, turning towards the newly
married couple, recites over them two long and beautiful prayers, as
follows:

"Be propitious, O Lord, unto our supplications, and graciously
assist thine own institutions, whereby thou hast ordained the
propagation of mankind, that what is joined together by thy
authority may be preserved through thy help. Through Jesus
Christ our Lord. Amen.

"O God, who, by the might of thy power, didst create all
things out of nothing; who, when the beginnings of the universe
had been set in order, and man had been made to the image of
God, didst ordain the inseparable assistance of woman, in such
wise that thou gavest beginning to her body out of the flesh of
man, teaching thereby that what it had pleased Thee should be
formed of one, it should never be lawful to put asunder: O God,
who hast consecrated the bond of matrimony by such an exceed-
ing mystery that in the covenant of marriage thou wouldst
signify the sacrament of Christ and his Church; O God, by whom
woman is joined to man, and society as ordained from the beginning is furnished with a blessing which alone was not re-

---

[1] In the Middle Ages, there was also, in certain places, a special Preface for the
Nuptial Mass, as follows: "It is truly meet and just, right and salutary, that we give
thee thanks always and in all places, holy Lord, almighty Father, who hast effected the
nuptial union with the sweet yoke of concord and the indissoluble bond of peace, in
order that the chaste fruitfulness of holy wedlock should be safeguarded by the procreation of adopted sons. For thy Providence, O Lord, and thy grace arranges in a
marvellous manner that what generation does for the beauty of the world, regeneration
should raise up to increase thy Church. And therefore, with angels and archangels,
with thrones and dominations, we sing a hymn to thy glory saying Holy, holy, holy. . . ."
(Cf. *Retours en Chrétienté*, by P. Doncoeur, Paris, Grasset, pp. 116-117). Similarly, in
some places there was a special *Hanc igitur* for the Nuptial Mass, as follows: "We
therefore beseech thee, O Lord, mercifully to accept this oblation of thy servants N.
and N., which they offer to thee on behalf of this thy servant here present, and we
beseech thy Majesty that, as thou hast brought her to a suitable age for wedlock, so
also, having joined her to her husband by thy favour, thou wilt complete her joy by
giving her the children she desires, and by guiding her in goodness, together with her
husband, in the space of life she wishes" (*Ibid.*, p. 117).

moved either in punishment of original sin or by the sentence of the Deluge: look mercifully upon this thy handmaid, who, being now to be joined in wedlock, earnestly desires to be fortified with thy protection. May it be to her a yoke of love and peace; may she marry in Christ, faithful and chaste, and remain a follower of holy women; may she be amiable to her husband like Rachel, wise like Rebecca, long-lived and faithful like Sara. In none of her deeds may that author of deceit have any power over her; may she abide firmly knit to the Faith and the commandments; united to one, may she fly from all that is unlawful; may she fortify her weakness by the strength of discipline; may she be in shamefacedness grave, in modesty venerable, in heavenly doctrines learned; may she be fruitful in offspring, approved and innocent; and attain unto the repose of the blessed and unto the heavenly kingdom, that they both may see their children's children unto the third and fourth generation, and arrive at the desired old age. Through the same Jesus Christ our Lord. Amen."

In many places it was the custom until comparatively recent times to cover the bridal pair at this point of the Mass with the "nuptial veil", a vestige of the *velamen sacerdotale* mentioned by St. Ambrose as being then used in the marriage ceremony.[1]

After the Agnus Dei, it was the custom for the husband to receive the kiss of peace from the priest at the altar, and then to give it to his bride. The first matrimonial kiss was thus sanctified in that it took place in the church itself before God's altar.[2]

After the Post-Communion prayer, and before the usual Blessing of the People, the priest turns to the bridegroom and bride, and imparts to them a solemn blessing, in these words:

"May the God of Abraham, Isaac and Jacob be with you; and fulfil his blessing abundantly upon you, that you may see your children's children to the third and fourth generation, and thereafter may you have life eternal without end, by the help of our Lord Jesus Christ, who with the Father and Holy Ghost liveth and reigneth, God, world without end. Amen."

Then the celebrant is instructed to give the newly-wedded couple a little homily, instructing them "to be ever faithful to one another; to keep chaste at times of prayer, and especially at fasts and great festivals; to love each other, and to live always in the fear of God."

Thereupon he sprinkles them with holy water.

---

[1] Cf. Doncoeur, *op. cit.*, p. 118.
[2] *Ibid.*, pp. 119-120.

The instruction to keep chaste was in former times much more definite and explicit, as we have seen.[1] And even in its present form, this rubric must be understood in the light of the universal teaching of modern theologians, who point out that there is no positive law of the Church forbidding the use of marriage on the night preceding the reception of Holy Communion, and that married people are not to be dissuaded from frequent communion because of their performance of the marriage act. We have seen how Pope Pius X condemned such attempts as "rigorism".[2] Hence, in its present form the rubric must be regarded as doing no more than counselling occasional abstinence from the conjugal act for religious motives, as recommended by St. Paul in *I Corinthians* vii, 5.[3]

The rubric does not specify abstinence now on the first three days after marriage, as recommended to Tobias by the Angel. This, as we have seen, was the subject of medieval church legislation whereby a bishop reserved to himself the power to grant a dispensation authorising the use of the marriage act on these particular nights.[4] We shall have more to say on this subject in a later chapter.

It is, of course, in every way desirable that the newly married couple should take all possible steps to obtain the full grace of the sacrament of matrimony by going to confession beforehand[5] and receiving Holy Communion in the Nuptial Mass itself, thus sanctifying their own bodies and souls, in preparation for their act of union, so soon to take place.

It is not generally known that, if for any reason the Nuptial Mass was omitted at the time of the wedding, it may take place at any time subsequently, provided both parties are Catholics and have not already received this solemn blessing of their nuptials. Further, those who are converted to the Catholic Faith after a valid marriage may then receive the Nuptial Blessing and have a Nuptial Mass celebrated.[6]

A Nuptial Mass cannot be celebrated if the marriage is a mixed one. Nor can the Nuptial Blessing be given if either of the parties was married before. But an exception is allowed if the husband alone

---

[1] See Part Two, p. 153.
[2] See Part One, p. 9.
[3] See Part Two, pp. 126–127.
[4] See Part Two, p. 153 and the article *Droit du Seigneur* in *Dict. Apol.*
[5] Those who receive the sacrament of matrimony in a conscious state of mortal sin do not at that time receive the specific grace of the sacrament, because of the existence of this obstacle. In addition, they are guilty of sacrilege. But once the obstacle (the state of mortal sin) has been removed by a good confession, the grace of the sacrament revives, according to the more common doctrine. In any case, whether received in a state of grace or not, the matrimonial bond which results from the contract comes into existence at once.
[6] See the rubrics of the *Rituale Romanum*, and O'Kane *Rubrics of the Roman Ritual*, p. 546.

has received the blessing previously: in that case the custom whereby the Nuptial Blessing is given to the wife in the second marriage may be retained.[1]

The Church's anxiety that her children should receive a special blessing when they marry is further exemplified by the fact that, if a Nuptial Mass cannot be celebrated, a special Nuptial Blessing may nevertheless be given, by Apostolic Indult, immediately after the marriage ceremony. This blessing consists of Psalm 127, *Beati omnes*; *Kyrie eleison*; the *Pater*, and a special prayer as follows:

"Bless, O Lord, and look down from Heaven upon this union, and as thou didst send thy holy angel Raphael peacefully to Tobias and Sara the daughter of Raguel, so also deign, O Lord, to send thy blessing upon these two persons joined in matrimony, that they may remain in thy benediction, persevere in thy will, and live in thy love. Through Jesus Christ our Lord. Amen."

Then the priest extends his hands over their heads, and blesses them, saying:

"May the Lord God Almighty bless you, and fulfil his benediction in you, and may you see the children of your children to the third and fourth generation, and reach the desired old age. Through Christ our Lord. Amen."

There is yet another Nuptial Blessing which may be used if the wife was married before and at that time received the Nuptial Blessing in the Mass, or again, if the marriage is being celebrated at a time when solemnities are not permitted. It consists of the same Psalm 127, *Pater, Kyrie*, and the following prayer:

"Stretch forth, we beseech thee, O Lord, the right hand of thy heavenly help upon these thy faithful, that they may seek thee with all their hearts, and obtain those things which they fittingly ask of thee. Through Christ our Lord. Amen."

An Apostolic Indult is required for the use of either of these special forms, but both are included in the *Ordo Administrandi* issued for England, and accordingly they may be used by any priest in the appropriate circumstances.[2]

Formerly the Church's part in the wedding did not end with the celebration of the Nuptial Mass, but there was a further beautiful and significant ceremony, namely, the Blessing of the Nuptial Bed.

[1] O'Kane, *op. cit.*, p. 547.
[2] See Fortescue-O'Connell, *Ceremonies of the Roman Rite*, 1943, p. 397; O'Connell, *General Rubrics of the Missal*, 1942, p. 93; Canon Mahoney in *Clergy Review*, June, 1945, pp. 171-172.

In the Sarum rite, the priest entered the bedchamber and said the following prayer:

"Bless, O Lord, and look down upon this chamber, O thou who sleepest not. Thou who watchest over Israel, protect thy servants who sleep in this bed, from all deceitful illusions of the wicked one. Keep them while they watch, that they may meditate upon thy precepts, and while they sleep, that they may find Thee in their slumbers, and that both here and everywhere they may be defended by thy assistance. Through Jesus Christ our Lord. Amen."

Then the priest blessed husband and wife, and incensed the bed, saying:

"May God bless your bodies and souls, and grant you the blessing which He gave to Abraham, Isaac and Jacob. Amen."

Such was the rite in our ancient English ritual.

It must not be thought that the blessing of the Nuptial Bed is altogether a thing of the past. The *Rituale Romanum*, even in its most modern edition, still has a "Blessing of the Bridal Bedchamber," as follows:

"Our help is in the name of the Lord,
Who hath made heaven and earth.
The Lord be with you,
And with thy spirit.
    Let us pray:
    Bless, O Lord, this bridal chamber, that those who dwell herein may remain together in thy peace, and continue in thy will, and grow old and be multiplied in length of days, and come to the heavenly kingdom. Through Christ our Lord. Amen."[1]

It is much to be regretted that, doubtless through a false prudery, this blessing of the marriage bedchamber is seldom if ever used nowadays. But certainly there would seem to be no good reason for refusing it to any enlightened Catholics who should ask for it.

---

[1] Here is the Latin text from the *Rituale Romanum*, Titulus VIII, cap. viii:
    Adjutorium nostrum in nomine Domini,
    Qui fecit caelum et terram.
    Dominus vobiscum.
    Et cum spiritu tuo.
        Oremus:
        Benedic, Domine, thalamum hunc, ut omnes habitantes in eo in tua pace consistant, et in tua voluntate permaneant, et senescant, et multiplicentur in longitudinem dierum, et ad regna caelorum perveniant.
    Per Christum Dominum nostrum. Amen.

CHAPTER EIGHT

THE SEX ACT AS AN EXPRESSION OF MUTUAL LOVE

WE have sufficiently explained in previous chapters that the primary object of marriage and of the sex act is the procreation of children. But one of the chief secondary objects is the expression of mutual love. Indeed, the celebration of the marriage, with its consecration of the affection of the spouses for each other, will naturally lead to the expression of this mutual love in the sex union. This aspect of the sex act deserves a special chapter to itself.

In animals, the sex act represents and expresses only the physical attraction and instinct of union as a means of reproduction, though it is certainly not impossible that, at least in the higher animals, the sex act is accompanied by some emotion and even affection. Man, however, is not only an animal: he is a *rational* animal, and this means that he is capable not only of sensitive love and affection but also of the higher kind of love which is seated in the human will. Husband and wife should be united, not only by emotion and affection of the sense order, but also by that higher love of the will. Indeed, this is implied in the injunction of St. Paul: "Husbands, love your wives, as Christ loved the Church" (*Ephes.*, v, 25). It must not, however, be inferred from this that the higher love is altogether separate from the lower: the two are united in man, and the higher love of the will is reflected and expressed in what Pope Pius XI calls "a deep-seated devotion of the heart."[1]

Now, all love desires and tends towards union with the object or person loved. And this is especially the case with matrimonial love. The two spouses have entered into the closest possible union—a union which should be one of mind and heart and soul as well as of bodies. The bodily union should serve precisely as a means of expression of this desire for perfect union. When the bodily union is thus linked up with the spiritual union of which it is the expression, its character is at once modified and elevated. The mere union of bodies as a result of sexual desire would seem to be motived by getting rather than by giving. This is seen especially in those unions which are precisely the expression of sensual lust. Love of the higher order, on the other hand, is characterised and motived, not by getting but by giving. The lover will do anything for the beloved;

---

[1] *Encyclical on Christian Marriage*, C.T.S. edn. p. 13.

he or she will willingly make any sacrifice, if it be for the sake of the one loved, and this sacrifice will testify to the reality and intensity of love. This desire to give can easily become a desire to surrender all that one has, and even one's very self to the other. And this mutual giving can receive its most suitable and concrete expression in the sex act. For in this, the husband gives himself to his wife, pouring into her body his own share of the source of life, and she in turn gives herself to her husband, freely and willingly offering herself to him for the act of union. Each gives himself or herself to the other, and each at the same time receives the other, in such a way that the two seem to merge into a perfect unity, and precisely that unity which is the aim of all true love. Thus, in this act of union, body and soul both take part, the union of the former being the means and the concrete expression of the union of the latter, which should therefore always accompany it.[1]

Viewed in this light, the sex act becomes at once a sublime and noble expression of mutual love, and essentially suitable for the divine choice as a symbol of the love between Christ and the Church.

There are, however, some difficulties in connection with the performance of the sex act which must form the subject of a warning. Love is, in a sense, an art which must be learnt, and love can always grow in its intensity and in its facility of expression. The newly married must be prepared for some difficulties, and even for imperfections and failures in the expression of their mutual love in the sex act, especially at first. The difficulties usually occur in the wife, though it is by no means unknown for the husband also to experience difficulties of his own. Normally, however, the husband finds it comparatively easy to consummate the sex union. But often there are serious difficulties on the part of the wife, both of a psychological and of a physical nature. The most obvious physical difficulty is the fact that the first marriage act will normally entail the breaking of the virginal hymen—an event which is often accompanied by some pain, and in any case involves some bleeding and consequent physical discomfort and soreness. A considerate husband will deal with his wife in this matter with the utmost tenderness and consideration. Were he to do otherwise, and proceed with precipitation and any lustful urgency, the effect on the wife might easily be to

[1] This union is beautfully expressed by Browning in the following words which a husband might use to his wife:
> "Because of our souls' yearning that we meet
> And mix in soul through flesh, which yours and mine
> Wear and impress, and make their visible selves,
> —All which means, for the love of you and me,
> Let us become one flesh, being one soul!"
> (*Ring and the Book*, Book VII, lines 774-778.)

generate a feeling of aversion and dislike for the sex act which it might take years to overcome. There may be other difficulties of a physiological nature, such as maladjustment, etc., but these can usually be remedied by a visit to a doctor.

On the wife's part, it is to be presumed that she understands that by the contract of matrimony she gives to her husband rights over her own body for the performance of the sex act, and that accordingly she will do her best to overcome any reluctance or physical difficulty which may arise.

The other difficulty which often occurs is mainly of a psychological nature. It results from the fact that, throughout girlhood and adolescence, there have grown up in the wife a series of inhibitions and repressions of anything connected with the sex instinct, which at first constitute an almost insuperable barrier to the proper and free and willing performance of the sex act. Sometimes these repressions result from an unwise education on sex matters, in which the act has been misrepresented as something essentially nasty and unclean. The effects of this disastrous kind of sex education may take some time to pass away, and in the meantime the wife may be at best a passive partner, and will not be able to correspond actively to her husband as she should do. Here, again, patience and consideration are absolutely necessary. The causes of these inhibitions and repressions should be clarified by a mutual exchange of ideas, and this will lead the way to their gradual disappearance, as right notions take the place of the former erroneous ones.

In any case, throughout the parties should adopt as a constant principle the fact that the sex act should always be preceded by acts of courtship and affection, and should never be begun without this preliminary preparation. These expressions of affectionate love, and acts of courtship, will sooner or later produce the desired effect, and make both parties ready and desirous for the act of union. Nature will see to that, once the inhibitions and repressions have been overcome. Even so, it may still happen that, for a time at least, the parties are unable to synchronise in the expression of their love. In that case, the one who has reached the climax—normally the husband—must do all that is possible to assist the other, just as one who has reached the top of a hill will stoop and lend a helping hand to pull up the other. In an Appendix to this chapter we give some general principles which should guide married folk in these difficult matters.

The subject just discussed is treated in most books on sex. Mr. Kenneth Walker, in his *Physiology of Sex*, p. 40, remarks:

"So belated is the orgasm in many (female) cases that it may only have been experienced once or twice during the whole of a woman's married life. . . . There are indeed many women, mothers of large families, who have never, during the whole of their long married life, experienced an orgasm. Some of these have undoubtedly been regarded as 'frigid' by their husbands, but their 'frigidity' is due solely to the fact that coitus has never continued long enough to secure for them complete sexual satisfaction. This difference in the latent period of the orgasm in the two sexes is the cause of many difficulties on the physical plane of marriage. Fortunately the trouble admits of remedy provided the husband is prepared to learn to be a better lover, and to supplement instinct by art."

As we have said, the difficulty can often be overcome by due preparation. In any case, it is one which must be foreseen, and dealt with in the best way possible. To leave it unsolved may render the whole married life an unhappy and dissatisfied one. Patience and tact are especially necessary here. As to patience, one has heard of a case in which all efforts to rouse and stimulate the wife met with failure until the first child was born. That seemed to unlock the mechanism, and finally to eradicate the results of years of inhibitions and repressions.

APPENDIX

By way of Appendix to this chapter, it will perhaps be useful if, without going into unnecessary details, we outline the teaching of Moral Theology concerning the morality of acts which lead up to or accompany the act of generation. The acts we have in mind are precisely those acts which would naturally occur in the "courtship" which, as we have said, should prepare and lead up to the sex union.

The first principle, then, is the following; *Whatever contributes in any way to the generation of a child is perfectly lawful.* Thus, kisses, touches, etc., etc., are all lawful as preparations for the act.

The second principle is the following; *Whatever is unrelated to the generation of a child, but is not against it, is not more than venially sinful, and it can be free from sin if performed for a good end such as the fostering of mutual love, etc.* This principle governs what are called "imperfect acts of love", such as embraces, kisses, touches, etc., when these are not intended to lead up to the sex act itself.

The third principle is this; *Whatever is against the generation of a child is gravely sinful.* This excludes the use of contraceptives, withdrawal, etc.

On questions of detail, or in any doubtful matter, the advice of a priest should be sought.

CHAPTER NINE

THE RELIGIOUS CHARACTER OF THE SEX ACT

THE sex act, then, is essentially a manifestation of the mutual love of husband and wife for each other—a love which will normally have its ultimate expression in the birth of offspring. Side by side with this, we find another and even more fundamental aspect of the sex act, namely, its *religious* character. This is unfortunately hardly ever realised, and it therefore calls for special consideration.

To assert that the sex act has a religious character will doubtless seem strange to those who have hitherto looked upon it merely as an animal act, yet it is clear that the sex act has indeed a religious character. This point has been made very clear by Pope Pius XI in his *Encyclical on Christian Marriage*. His Holiness says:

"Clearly, the offspring begotten by God's almighty power with the co-operation of husband and wife is a very noble gift of His goodness, and a most excellent fruit of marriage. Christian parents should understand, moreover, that their duty is not only to propagate and maintain the human race on earth: it is not even merely to rear worshippers of the true God. They are called to give children to the Church, to beget fellow-citizens of the Saints and members of the household of God, in order that the worshippers of our God and Saviour may increase from day to day."[1]

Thus, parents act in the first place as God's instruments in propagating the human race on earth. Secondly, they have the duty to bring into the world new worshippers of the true God. And thirdly, their office is to bring into being new members of the Church, which is the Mystical Body of Christ. And all this is brought about precisely by the performance of the sex act, and cannot happen without it. Here we have abundant grounds for asserting the religious character of the sex act itself. First, then, it is a marvellous function, in which human beings are given to share in the creative work of God Himself. Secondly, it is the means of increasing the worshippers of the true God. And thirdly, it is the divinely ordained means of growth of the Mystical Body of Christ. To all this add the fact, asserted in Holy Scripture, that marriage is a sign of the union

[1] C.T.S. edn., p. 9.

between Christ and the Church, precisely inasmuch as it is consummated in the sex union whereby two beings become one flesh, and there is then surely no room for doubt as to the sacred and religious character of the sex act, performed in the manner in which God ordained it.

Hence, the performance of the sex act may well be regarded as itself a religious function. If St. Paul exhorts us to do all things, whether we eat or drink, to the glory of God, surely married people can perform the sex act also for the honour and glory of God. The knowledge that they are acting as instruments of God's creative power, and in accordance with His laws, and for His own purposes, must heighten this religious character of the act. It is doubtless the clearer realisation of this fact that has led the authorities of the Church in recent times to insist that there is no need for married people to abstain from receiving Holy Communion after performing the sex act. Indeed, in itself, it would seem essentially right and proper that those who have, by joining themselves to each other in the sex act, given, as it were, a sacramental illustration of the union between Christ and the Church, should proceed as soon as possible to receive the real Sacrament of Unity, whereby Christ unites himself to our souls, and ourselves to Him, in such a way that we become "members of His body, of His flesh and of His bones."[1]

What, then are we to say of the prohibition in previous times of the approach to the altar by married persons who used their rights and privileges? This must, we think, be explained by the widespread belief in those times that the sex act was always more or less sinful, or at least that there was always a possibility of sin accompanying the sex act, and further, by the fact that, even apart from any question of sin, the sex act in fallen man tends to cloud the reason, at least at the time of its performance, in such a way that, at that particular moment, it seems impossible to think of God and divine things, and for some time afterwards one seems to be drawn to earthly things rather than to divine. This feature of the sex act, however, is, as St. Thomas Aquinas has explained, a penalty of original sin, and is not in itself sinful.[2] Moreover, as we have seen,[3] passion has its rightful part to play in the performance of the act. Even so, human nature is so weak that there remains always a possibility that the performance of the sex act has been dictated, not by lofty moral and religious considerations, but merely for the sake of the physical satisfaction of the sex urge, or only for the sake of the pleasure attached. And such an intention can, as we have seen,[4]

---

[1] *Ephesians*, v. 30.
[2] See Part Two, pp. 177–179.
[3] See Part Two, pp. 177–179.
[4] See Part Two, pp. 175–176.

easily involve sin, especially if it is so intense that it even involves an exclusion of the primary end of marriage and of the sex act.

On the other hand, we must never forget that, when rightly exercised for the proper intentions, the performance of the sex act, so far from being sinful, or at least indifferent, is in fact meritorious in the strict theological sense of the word. That is, it is an act which, being performed in a state of grace, merits further graces, and in company with other works performed in a state of grace, helps us to merit eternal life itself. This is so important that it seems worth while to give the passage in which St. Thomas Aquinas sets it forth. It comes from the *Summa Theologica*, III Suppl., q. 41, art. 4:

> "Since no act proceeding deliberately from the will is in-different, the matrimonial act is always either sinful or meritorious in one possessing grace. For, if one is led to perform the marriage act, either by the virtue of justice, in order to render the debt, or by the virtue of religion, that children may be procreated for the worship of God, the act is meritorious."[1]

Thus, the performance of the sex act in the right way and for the right intention becomes an exercise of the virtue of religion itself, and therefore a religious act. One will look in vain, however, in the works of modern moral theologians, for any such doctrine. It is surely time to return to St. Thomas in this matter![2]

---

[1] "Cum nullus actus ex deliberata voluntate procedens sit indifferens . . . actus matrimonialis semper est peccatum vel meritorius in eo qui gratiam habet. Si enim ad actum matrimonialem virtus inducat vel justitiae, ut debitum reddat, vel religionis, ad proles ad cultum Dei procreetur, est meritorius."

[2] The nearest approach to this doctrine is the statement by Father Henry Davis in his *Moral and Pastoral Theology*, Vol. IV, p. 243, that "sexual intercourse . . . is lawful, honourable, morally good, and may be meritorious". Similar statements may be found in other good theologians, such as Vermeersch. But neither Father Davis nor Père Vermeersch say expressly that the sex act is an act of the virtue of religion, when per-formed in the right way by married people. Yet that is precisely the doctrine of St. Thomas. While ignored by moral theologians, it has been duly set forth by Father Hugh Pope, O.P., in his note to *I Corinthians* vii, 6, in his *Layman's New Testament*, but without any emphasis: "The use of marriage . . . may be meritorious and absolutely sinless; if for the sake of having children who are to be brought up in the fear of God it is an act of religion. . . ." (p. 579).

CHAPTER TEN

WHEN SHOULD SEXUAL INTERCOURSE TAKE PLACE?

WE can now usefully turn to the question when sexual intercourse should take place. In view of what has been said in a previous chapter concerning the breaking of the virginal hymen, and the psychological difficulties experienced by many women in the first stages of this important and far-reaching change in their lives, it will be realised that, even from this standpoint alone, there is much to be said for the old practice recommended in the *Book of Tobias* and adhered to by many Catholics, especially in the Middle Ages, namely, abstaining from the act for the first three nights after the marriage. The Scriptural account of Tobias's actions deserves to be pondered:

"The angel Raphael said to Tobias: '. . . They who in such manner receive matrimony as to shut out God from themselves and from their mind, and to give themselves to their lust, as the horse and mule which have not understanding, over them the devil hath power. But thou, when thou shalt take her, go into thy chamber, and for three days keep thyself continent with her, and give thyself to nothing else but to prayers with her. . . . And the third night thou shalt obtain a blessing that sound children may be born of you. And when the third night is past, thou shalt take the virgin with the fear of the Lord, moved rather for love of children than for lust, that in the seed of Abraham thou mayest obtain a blessing in children."

We read that, after the wedding: [1]

"Tobias exhorted the virgin and said to her: 'Sara, arise, and let us pray to God to-day and to-morrow and the next day: because for these three nights we are joined to God: and when the third night is over, we will be in our own wedlock. For we are the children of saints, and we must not be joined together like heathens that know not God.' So they both arose, and prayed earnestly both together that health might be given them."[2]

[1] *Tobias* vi, 17-22, according to the Douay Version, based on the Vulgate which follows an Aramaic original. The three nights abstinence is not mentioned in the Greek MSS. of Tobias.
[2] *Tobias* viii, 4-6.

Holy Scripture goes on to give the substance of their petitions:

"Tobias said: 'Lord God of our fathers, may the heavens and the earth, and the sea and the fountains, and the rivers, and all thy creatures that are in them, bless thee. Thou madest Adam of the slime of the earth, and gavest him Eve for a helper. And now, Lord, thou knowest that not for fleshly lust do I take my sister to wife, but only for the love of posterity, in which thy name may be blessed for ever and ever.'

"Sara also said: 'Have mercy on us, O Lord, have mercy on us, and let us grow old both together in health.' "[1]

Finally, the book records that the marriage was indeed blessed by God, and Tobias lived to see his children and his children's children to the fifth generation.

If the sex act is treated in a similar religious way, it will in no wise lessen its delight, but rather, the religious joy of doing God's will will be added to the physical and mental pleasure of the act of union.

Even to this day, in some parts of Brittany it is customary to consecrate the first night of married life to the Blessed Virgin, and the second to St. Joseph. But this practice, though it may be recommended, must depend upon the mutual agreement of the spouses, and is in no sense a precept. It may therefore be disregarded without any sin.

The *frequency* of the marriage act, especially in the early days, must be a matter of mutual arrangement and consent. As the essence of the marriage contract is the giving to the other party of rights over one's own body, it follows that the act must be performed as often as the other party reasonably desires it, and to do otherwise, and refuse the marriage debt, is to commit a mortal sin against justice, as St. Thomas Aquinas implies in a passage already quoted.[2] If this important truth were more widely known and realised, there would perhaps be less unhappiness in married life. The husband in particular must remember that it is not normal for a woman to request directly the rendering of the debt, but she can and doubtless will give signs and indications which a discerning and loving husband will know how to interpret.

It may happen, of course, that the desire is at first present only in one of the two parties, and in that case, care must be taken to prepare the other party in the way suggested in a previous chapter, so that

[1] *Tobias* viii, 7-10.
[2] See p. 33.

the act, though originally desired by one party alone, finally becomes the wish of both.

In all this matter of sex life, both parties must try to exercise due moderation. The use of sex should be a rational act, and thus it should be brought under the control of reason so far as possible. In any case, to act in an unreasonable manner, or to become the slave of sensual appetites, would sooner or later destroy all real joy in the sex act. This fact in itself will prevent the too frequent performance of it. Physical grounds, and the weariness or even exhaustion which often follow a too intemperate sex life, will also dictate prudence and care in this matter. And finally, we have the advice of St. Paul: "Deprive not one another, unless it be by consent, for a time, that you may devote yourselves to prayer, and then be together again, lest Satan use your lack of self-control to tempt you" (*I Corinthians* vii, 5).

We now come to some particular questions. *Intercourse during the menstrual period* was strictly forbidden in the Old Testament law, even under pain of death (*Leviticus* xv, 19-20; xx, 18). It has been suggested that this may have been motived by the fact that in those hot regions the menstrual flow was often great, that some of the blood might be more or less corrupted, and that contact with it might lead to disease.[1] However this may be, it is certainly true that, as recent research has shown, conception is normally impossible during that time, and it was the divine intention that the Jews should be as fruitful as possible. As for the present time, while there may be little or no risk of disease, there is often a certain reluctance in wives to permit the act when they are in this condition—a reluctance which is easily understandable, and should be respected. Some theologians consider it venially sinful to have intercourse at this time.

The next question which arises is that of *intercourse during pregnancy*. The difficulty here is that it may easily be two months before there is any solid foundation for thinking that a woman is pregnant. Thus, there are two points to consider. First, can intercourse continue until it is certain that a woman is pregnant? And secondly, should intercourse continue once it is established that a woman is pregnant? It will be more convenient to discuss this second question first. We have seen that in earlier times intercourse was forbidden under these circumstances, doubtless because of the risk, real or supposed, of inducing abortion. Medical authorities at the present time do not speak with one voice on this matter. One writer says:

"There is no doubt that the uterine contractions which

1 Cf. Eschbach, *Disputationes Physiologico-Theologicae*, p. 122.

accompany strenuous coitus can provoke a miscarriage. As we know, female animals avoid all contact with the male while they bear their young. This would seem to indicate that Nature is opposed to sexual intimacy during pregnancy."[1]

On the other hand, another writer says:

"From the medical standpoint, it may be said that during the first five months of pregnancy, sexual intercourse is not harmful to healthy women, and in particular there is no danger of miscarriage during these months, unless sexual intercourse is performed violently. . . . From the sixth to the eighth month, however, sexual abstinence becomes more and more necessary, and from the eighth month onward abstinence must be complete."[2]

According to the "Mothercraft" system initiated and developed by the late Sir F. Truby King, and widely practised in Australia and New Zealand, abstinence is enjoined "during the first three months, and the last two months of pregnancy", and in addition, "sexual relations should also be avoided during the time when the wife would normally have her monthly period", in order to avoid any possibility of miscarriage.[3]

Modern theologians generally assert that intercourse during pregnancy is lawful, provided it is moderate, and that care is taken to avoid any danger to the fœtus. The greater the danger, the more care must be taken, and thus complete abstinence may be indicated towards the end of the pregnancy.

We can now turn back to the other question, that of intercourse continuing until pregnancy is certain. Theologians in general have no hesitation in allowing intercourse to continue during this period. But there are some medical considerations which, it seems, should be taken into consideration here.

Those who are experienced in such matters are of the opinion that it is quite easy to disturb an already developing fertilised ovum by the motions which often accompany intercourse, and in this way it is possible that many conceptions may fail to come to term. This is not without its importance. Many people who desire a child have intercourse several times during the period in which conception is likely, and continue to do so, at any rate unless and until signs of pregnancy manifest themselves. They do not realise that by this frequent intercourse they may be defeating their own object, and

---

[1] *Encyclopædia of Sex*, p. 514.
[2] *Pastoral Medicine*, by Rev. Dr. Ruland, p. 23.
[3] *Mothercraft*, by Mary Truby King, p. 27.

preventing the development of conceptions which have already taken place. The difficulty is that there is no evidence that conception has taken place, until some weeks have elapsed. Hence one can only recommend that, if a child is desired, and intercourse takes place say once or twice during the "likely" period, one should then abstain for a time, or at least until the absence of any definite signs makes it manifest that in fact no conception has as yet taken place.

As to *intercourse after childbirth*, one authority writes as follows:

"After birth, complete abstinence must be practised for at least four weeks. From the fourth, and certainly from the sixth week, sexual intercourse may be resumed. Unfortunately, experience teaches that many men do not accord their wives the proper consideration in this matter" (Ruland, *Pastoral Medicine*, p. 24).

Others would confine the period of abstinence to two weeks after birth. Probably the period varies in different cases.

One thing is clear: the husband will certainly have to abstain completely from sexual intercourse during the time immediately before and after childbirth, and this may easily mean abstinence for at least two months. The self-control which is indicated here may be difficult, but it is certainly not impossible, and it will be all the easier if the parties have been accustomed to practise a certain amount of self-control at other periods in their married life.

Intercourse is quite lawful *during the change of life*, and *afterwards*. This, and the fact that intercourse is lawful during the early months of pregnancy, may seem to require explanation. For how can the act be lawful at these times, seeing that it is quite impossible for it to bring about what we have described as the "primary end" of the sex act, namely, the procreation of children? The answer to this is that the act itself is still being performed in a way which is, of itself, capable of generating offspring. The parties performing the act are interposing no obstacle in the way of the attainment of the primary end. The obstacle, such as it is, is the work of Nature itself, and the presence of an already fertilised ovum. It would be wrong for human beings to take steps to hinder conception, but it is not wrong for Nature itself to make a conception impossible. We must deal with this in exactly the same way as we should deal with the question of the taking of human life. It is wrong to take human life (except in those special circumstances in which we deem that God has given us his authority to do so, as in the case of the execution of murderers, etc., by the State). Thus, it is wrong to kill anyone, even though he or she may be suffering from an incurable disease. True, all men must die sooner or later, and will die. But their death is inflicted by Nature, and therefore by God, the Author of Nature and the Sovereign Lord of Life and Death. We must not assume to ourselves His divine right and power.

Hence, those performing the sex act at times when conception is impossible, are not themselves placing any obstacle to the normal consequences of the act: the obstacle is put there by Nature itself, and therefore by Nature's God.

Moreover, this obstacle prevents the attainment only of the primary end. The secondary ends of the marriage act, namely, the fostering of mutual love, and the abatement of concupiscence, are still attained by the act. Thus, on the one hand the primary end is not being deliberately excluded or prevented by human endeavour, and on the other hand the secondary ends are still being attained. And for these reasons, the act is legitimate at the times in question.

The same reasoning applies to the performance of the act during the period when, according to modern medical opinion, conception is extremely unlikely, if not impossible, i.e., just after and just before menstruation.[1]

The principles just explained have been authoritatively adopted and set forth by Pope Pius XI in his *Encyclical on Christian Marriage*. Here we read:

"Husband and wife are not to be accused of acting against nature if they make use of their right in a proper and natural manner, even though natural causes (due to circumstances of time, or to certain defects) render it impossible for new life to originate. Both matrimony and the use of the matrimonial right have secondary ends—such as mutual help, the fostering of reciprocal love, and the abatement of concupiscence—which husband and wife are quite entitled to have in view, so long as the intrinsic nature of that act, and therefore its due subordination to its primary end, is safeguarded."[2]

---

[1] For details of this "safe period", see works by Dr. Halliday Sutherland, *Laws of Life* and *Control of Life*, and our later chapter on Birth Control.
[2] C.T.S. edn., p. 27.

CHAPTER ELEVEN

THE RELIGIOUS ASPECT OF PREGNANCY

It should not be long after marriage before the wife confides lovingly to her husband her great secret—that she is becoming a mother. What tender thoughts must fill both husband and wife at this time, if they have a right view of marriage and its blessings! And how different from the expressions of regret, and the mutual recriminations of which one sometimes hears!

One thing is certain: the Church regards with especial tenderness the woman who is about to become a mother. In England a woman is then said to be "in a certain condition". In Ireland it is more usual to say that she is in "a blessed condition".

There is, in the Roman Ritual, a special blessing which the Church offers to a pregnant woman, where there is any doubt as to her safety. It is a beautiful rite, and is not so well known as it should be. The Roman Ritual contemplates its use only when there is danger in childbirth. But it should be known that the Holy See has granted to many of the Catholic Bishops of England and Wales[1] authority for its use in all cases of conception. This grant was made in reply to a special petition sent to the Holy See by the late Cardinal Bourne, setting forth the fact that:

"In our days, anti-conceptive views are so strong that it seems opportune, and even necessary, that Catholic wives should be helped and fortified by spiritual aids, so that they may with generous hearts take up the burden of motherhood."

The privilege of using the form in the Roman Ritual for all cases of pregnancy was granted by the Sacred Congregation of Rites in 1928. Here is an English translation of this form:

"Our help is in the name of the Lord,
Who hath made heaven and earth.
Save thy handmaid, O Lord,
Who hopeth in thee, O my God.
Be unto her, O Lord, a tower of strength
From the face of the enemy.

[1] Cf. Canon Mahoney, in *Clergy Review*, Dec. 1942, p. 561, and May 1945, p. 225.

Let not the enemy prevail against her,
Nor the son of iniquity approach to hurt her.
Send her help, O Lord, from the sanctuary,
And defend her out of Sion.
O Lord, hear my prayer,
And let my cry come unto thee.
The Lord be with you,
And with thy spirit.
  Let us pray.
Almighty, everlasting God, who hast given to thy servants, in the confession of the true Faith, to acknowledge the glory of the eternal Trinity, and in the power of majesty to adore the Unity; grant, we beseech thee, that, by steadfastness in the same Faith, this thy handmaid may ever be defended from all adversities. Through Christ our Lord. Amen.
  Let us pray.
Lord God, Creator of all things, strong and terrible, just and merciful, who alone art good and kind; who deliveredst Israel from all evil; who madest our fathers beloved by thee, and didst sanctify them by the power of thy Spirit; who, by the co-operation of the Holy Spirit, didst prepare the body and soul of the glorious Virgin Mary that she might be worthy to be made a fitting habitation for thy Son; who madest John the Baptist to be filled with the Holy Spirit, and to leap in his mother's womb; accept the sacrifice of a contrite heart, and the fervent desire of thy handmaid, who humbly beseecheth thee for the preservation of the offspring which thou hast given her to conceive; take care of this woman, who is thine, and defend her from all craft and injury of the direful enemy; that, by the helping hand of thy mercy, her offspring may come prosperously to the light of day, may be preserved for holy regeneration, may evermore serve thee in all things, and merit to attain unto everlasting life. Through the same Christ our Lord. Amen."

Then the woman is sprinkled with holy water, and the 66th Psalm is said:

"God, be merciful unto us, and bless us;
Cause the light of his countenance to shine upon us,
  And have mercy on us,
That we may know thy way upon earth;
Thy salvation in all nations.
Let the people praise thee, O God:
Let all the people praise thee.

O let the nations be glad and rejoice;
For thou dost judge the people with justice,
And govern the nations upon earth.
Let the people praise thee, O God;
Let all the people praise thee:
The earth hath yielded her fruit.
May God, even our own God, bless us,
May God bless us:
And may all the ends of the earth fear Him.
Glory be to the Father, etc."

Then come the following versicles, responses and prayer:

"Let us bless the Father and the Son with the Holy Spirit,
Let us praise and highly exalt him for ever.
God hath given his angels charge concerning thee,
To keep thee in all thy ways.
O Lord, hear my prayer,
And let my cry come unto thee.
The Lord be with you,
And with thy spirit.
Let us pray.
Visit, we beseech thee, O Lord, this habitation, and drive all dangers far from it, and from this thy handmaid: let thy holy angels dwell herein, who may keep her and her offspring in peace; and let thy blessing be always upon her: save them, O almighty God, and grant unto them thy perpetual light. Through our Lord Jesus Christ, etc."

Lastly, the rite concludes with a special blessing for the mother and her child:

"May the blessing of God almighty, of the Father, and of the Son, and of the Holy Ghost, descend upon thee and upon thine offspring, and abide for ever. Amen."

There would seem to be in some places a custom whereby an expectant mother goes to the priest and asks him to bless her breasts, that she may be able to produce a good supply of milk for her future child. The breasts are blessed, apparently, by making the sign of the Cross upon them. I have not been able to obtain any information as to the prayers, if any, which are said at the blessing, and there is certainly no form for any such blessing in the *Rituale Romanum*.
A Catholic woman must, alas! be prepared to meet with dis-

approving glances from some of her friends—and even from some co-religionists—when they recognise her condition, especially if she already has some children. Such a mother might well take comfort from the following verses, written by Miss Doris Burton:

> A pregnant woman passed close by.
> "O what a sight!"
> I heard two drawling voices say,
> "Why, in that plight
> She should not horrify,
> But hide away
> Till evening late,
> The ugliness of woman in that state."
>
> A pregnant woman passed close by.
> O wondrous sight!
> Within her womb the Child she bore
> That Christmas night
> Deigned thus to sanctify
> For evermore—
> Through this her grace—
> The motherhood of all the human race.[1]

---

[1] *The Incarnation and Other Poems*, by Doris Burton, Ilfracombe: Arthur Stockwell. p. 21.

CHAPTER TWELVE

THE CHURCH AND CHILDBIRTH

ONCE the child is born, it should be baptised as soon as possible. This rite is fairly familiar to all, and need not be described here. Thereby the newly born infant is made a child of God, a member of the Church, and an heir to the Kingdom of Heaven. Original sin is washed away, and in the case of an adult who is being baptised, any other sin which may have been committed, provided an act of sorrow has been made. And lastly, the soul is filled with sanctifying grace, and especially clothed with the virtues of faith, hope and charity.

Even this does not end the Church's generous care of the child. For the Roman Ritual contains further rites: *The Blessing of an Infant; The Blessing of a Child; The Blessing of Children when they are presented in Church;* and *The Blessing of Children who are Sick.*

But the Church, in her care for the child, does not forget the mother. For there is a rite which is called in the present Roman Ritual *The Churching of Women.* This rite corresponds to the old custom in the Jewish Law whereby, at the end of a period of "uncleanness" following childbirth, the mother was "purified" by a ceremony in the Temple and the offering of a sacrifice for sin. By a sublime act of condescension and obedience to the Jewish Law, Our Blessed Lady went thus to the Temple in Jerusalem to be "purified" after the birth of the child Jesus—and this event the Church celebrates on the Feast of the Purification, February 2nd.

In some old liturgical books, such as those of the Sarum rite, the ceremony of the Churching of Women is similarly called *The Purification of Women after Childbirth,* and it was similarly called a "Purification" in the Statutes of the diocese of Cashel and Emly drawn up in 1782.[1]

There is, therefore, presumably some sense in which this Christian rite may still be called a "purification". The Jewish Law has, of course, been abrogated completely so far as its ceremonial code is concerned, and equally, all the old legal prescriptions concerning ritual purity, clean and unclean animals, etc., have been abolished. And hence, even the ritual stain which, in the Old Testament

---

[1] See the books of the Sarum Rite, and also O'Kane, *Rubrics of the Roman Ritual,* 1932, pp. 264-265. The ancient *Canons of Hippolytus* similarly called the ceremony of "Purification".

legislation, was attached to childbirth, is no longer recognised. We have seen that, even in the Old Testament, childbirth as such could not have been regarded as immoral or sinful. But we have also seen that, both in conception and in childbirth, there may be some minor sins: sins of passion in the act of generation, or wrong intention, and sins of impatience and rebellion in the act of birth. Moreover, both in the Jewish and also in the Christian dispensations, children are born without the grace of God, and are, in that sense, "children of wrath", with the stain of original sin on their souls. Finally, there are still the physical consequences of childbirth, which cause a mother to feel, in a sense, uncomfortable. For all these reasons, the Christian rite may also be called a "purification" from any sin or stain which may be attached to childbirth in the sense explained. Doubtless it is this idea which has led the Church to indicate, in the rubrics of the rite, that the woman is to stay in the porch of the church, or by the door, until the priest comes to bless her by sprinkling holy water.

But, while the note of purification need not be altogether excluded from this rite,[1] its predominant note is, not purification but thanks-giving. The introductory rubric speaks of a woman after child-birth "desiring, according to pious and praiseworthy custom, to come to the church and give thanks to God for her safe delivery, and to ask for a blessing from the priest." Accordingly, after the recitation of Psalm 23, the woman is led into the church by the priest, who says to her: "Enter into the temple of God; adore the Son of the Blessed Virgin Mary, who in offspring hath given thee fruitfulness." When the altar is reached, there are a number of versicles and responses, and finally a special prayer of thanksgiving:

"Almighty everlasting God, who, through the delivery of the Blessed Virgin Mary, hast turned to joy the pains of the faith-ful in childbirth, look mercifully on thy servant, who comes in gladness to thy temple to return thanks, and grant that, after this life, by the merits and intercession of the same Blessed Mary, she may prove worthy to attain, with her offspring, to the joys of everlasting happiness."

Thus does the Church consecrate the sacred office of motherhood,

[1] Strangely enough, Father Martindale, in the Catholic Truth Society edition of the *Rite of Churching*, considers it "a pity that the idea that this service is some sort of purification from I know not what taint, falsely supposed to have been incurred in childbirth, is said to exist here and there." He adds that "no such taint, nor any taint, is incurred by what is, in truth, a privilege and a glory." But surely, motherhood can be in itself "a privilege and a glory", and yet also be accompanied by some sin and imperfection?

and link up the motherhood of Christian women with the mother-hood of the Blessed Virgin Mary.

Sometimes, alas! a married couple is disappointed, and God does not deign to bless their union with a child. In such circumstances, in times past the Church suggested special prayers, which could be used in the Sacrifice of the Mass itself. Here are the prayers found for the purpose in the Gelasian Sacramentary. Though they no longer appear in our modern Missals, they might certainly be used for the private devotion of a woman who desires a child but has so far been disappointed:

"O God, who didst deign to fecundate through Abraham the sterile womb of Sara, so that, against all hope, he should have descendants, mercifully regard the prayers of thy servant N., who pleads her sterility before thee: give her, as thou didst to our fathers, fruitfulness, and bless the children whom thou mayest grant to her.

"O God, who didst deign to hear thy servant Isaac, who pleaded before thee the sterility of his marriage, and didst grant to Rebecca to become a mother, mercifully hear the prayers of thy servant N., who asks a child from thee, so that the firm hope which she has put in thy mercy may be crowned by the gift which she implores through Our Lord Jesus Christ.

"O God, who by delivering Rachel from the reproach of sterility, didst grant her fecundity while she was anxiously begging from thee that she should become a mother, mercifully grant to thy servant N. the joy of being fruitful amongst women who have pleased thee, and to obtain that which she asks with faith from thy goodness.

"Eternal almighty God, who didst change into joy the groanings of Anna by rendering her fruitful, mercifully fulfil the desire of thy servant N. to be fruitful, and for the praise of thy glory remove from her the reproach of sterility.

"O God, who didst will the sterility of Elizabeth in the hidden design that she should one day become fruitful at the voice of an angel, mercifully grant that, as Elizabeth conceived the Fore-runner of the Lord in the midst of the Jewish people, so also thy servant N. may have a son, who may serve thee by increasing the faith of this people.

"O God, who, regarding mercifully the sorrow of sterile women, dost miraculously give them fruitfulness, even when they despair, mercifully grant to thy servant N. to obtain through thy servant Gregory the fruitfulness which she cannot obtain alone.

"O eternal almighty God, who didst not refuse to the most holy Mary ever a Virgin to be a mother, and to generate Our Saviour, mercifully grant to thy servant N., through the prayers of the same Mother of God, to merit to become herself a mother."

Here is the corresponding Secret Prayer for the Mass:

"Accept, O Lord, our prayers, with the offering of these sacrifices, which we offer to thy clemency with a suppliant heart, on behalf of thy servant N., and since thou hast created so strong a desire in the heart of women to become mothers, remove from her the sorrow of being unfruitful, and mercifully bless her, so that she may have a child."

And lastly, here is the Post-Communion prayer:

"Having received the gift of heavenly life, we pray thee, O almighty God, that what we have asked for thy servant N. we may merit to see accorded to her, through thy mercy."

CHAPTER THIRTEEN

THE SIZE OF THE FAMILY

WE must now consider another aspect of married life, and that is the question of the number of children in the family. We may freely admit that in the past several Fathers and Doctors of the Church have seemed to deprecate the procreation of many children, and have unduly insisted upon St. Paul's statement, "the time is short; it remaineth that they who have wives be as if they had none" (*I Corinthians* viii, 29).[1]

St. Augustine, for instance, wrote that "in the case of the patriarchs, whose mission it was to increase and conserve the people of God, the propagation of children was indeed most commendable; but now it is no longer a necessity. Since the time of Jesus Christ, the chief duty is to regenerate spiritually those children who are born in any way throughout all the nations. These words of Scripture, 'There is a time to embrace, and a time to abstain from all embraces' (*Eccles*. iii, 5), perfectly describe for us these two periods in the world's history. The first period is that which preceded Jesus Christ; the second is that which has followed his coming." And again: "Seeing that Christ does not now demand that we should prepare for his coming by multiplying the family, would it not be foolish to expose oneself to this 'tribulation of the flesh' which constitutes marriage, unless there is reason to fear most deplorable falls through incontinence, as a result of the temptations of the devil?"[2]

Even as late as the eighteenth and nineteenth centuries, treatises of Moral Theology were on the whole opposed to the idea that there could be any positive "duty to marry", or that, in marriage itself, there could be any "duty to procreate children", and spiritual writers seem to have emphasised temperance and chastity rather than the precept in *Genesis*, "Increase and multiply". Thus, about 1844, Mgr. Gousset, described as "one of the theological glories of the French episcopate" and successively Bishop of Perigueux,

---

[1] This statement of St. Paul should of course be considered in the light of others in the same chapter: "Art thou bound to a wife? seek not to be loosed" (v. 27). "If thou take a wife, thou hast not sinned" (v. 28). "Defraud not one another, except perhaps by consent for a time . . . and return together again" (v. 5).

[2] These passages are quoted from St. Augustine by P. Méline in his *Morale Familiale*, p. 105.

Archbishop of Rheims, and Cardinal, wrote a textbook of *Moral Theology for Parochial Clergy and Confessors*, in which he championed the view that the human race was already sufficiently numerous.[1] And even Taperelli, described by Mr. A. C. F. Beales as "the greatest of all Catholic Internationalists,"[2] actually went so far as to suggest that authority should endeavour to "moderate the excessive multiplication of marriages."[3] Hence it is not surprising to read that as recently as 1915, one good Catholic mother could say to her daughter: "If you have a second child—an event which I hope will not take place. . . ."[4]

It would seem on the whole that the fault of these ancient and modern writers has been to concentrate almost exclusively on the question of individual rights and duties, to the almost complete exclusion of the *social* character and function of marriage, in marked distinction to the great medieval Scholastics. It is quite true, of course, that the precept "Increase and multiply" is one which is addressed to the human race as a whole rather than to any particular individuals, and St. Thomas Aquinas himself made use of this when justifying the abstention from marriage by those who choose celibacy for God's honour and glory—and also be it noted, for the sake of society.[5] But equally, the celibacy of the few is justified precisely by the fact that the others give themselves to the duty of propagating the human race, and it is surely very difficult for those who choose the married state to evade the force of this precept, or to maintain that it does not apply to them. Why, then, do they marry, if not to have children?[6]

Not all members of the community are called to the married state, though doubtless this is the vocation of the majority. Even so, not all marriages are fruitful, and not all children survive to adult age. This being the case, it must be evident to anyone who will reflect for a moment, that even two children of each marriage will not suffice to keep the population at its present strength, much less to increase it. If every married couple produce two children who survive to adult age, then certainly the father and mother have reproduced themselves. But this makes no allowance whatever for the lack of fecundity in those who, for one reason or another, either do not or cannot produce two children as a result of their marriage, and again, it fails to provide for the replacement of those

[1] Méline, *ibid.*, p. 103.
[2] *Catholic Church and International Order*, p. 109.
[3] Cf. Méline, *op. cit.*, p. 104.
[4] *Ibid.*, p. 104.
[5] See passage quoted on pp. 13–14.
[6] St. Thomas says expressly that those whose duty it is to see to the propagation of the race do not laudably abstain from sex pleasures (IIa IIae, q. 152, art. 1, ad. 2).

others who do not marry at all. And note that so far we are dealing only with the *conservation* of the race, not with its *increase*. To fulfil the precept "Increase and multiply", we may reasonably say that *at least four children should be produced by those who are able to do so*. Even then, the rate of increase will not be very great.

Married people should surely remember that the married state is precisely their *vocation*, and that the primary end of marriage, as well as of the marriage act, is the procreation of children. That is why Pope Pius XI says that "among the blessings of marriage, offspring holds the first place."[1] Again, the Pope does not hesitate to speak of the "duty" of Christian parents in this matter: "Christian parents should understand that their *duty* is, not only to propagate and maintain the human race on earth . . . they are called upon to give children to the Church."[2]

All this is confirmed by the manifest evils of one-child families, which are found also to a lesser degree in families with only two children. The companionship of other children is an essential part of their moral, spiritual and physical education, and where can this companionship be better found than in the bosom of the family itself? The parent has no control over other people's children, but one can watch for any undesirable development in one's own. This does not mean that children should be denied other playmates: quite the contrary. But these others should be supplementary to the members of one's own family, and not substitutes for these.

We must not, however, leave this subject without dealing with a very real objection which is constantly being urged against large families. Is it really the Catholic view that parents should all have large families, irrespective of their financial circumstances and economic prospects? Have not parents a duty to do their best to the child or children they already have, and does not this duty itself require that the family should not be further increased, but should from now on be limited, so that the existing children may be brought up properly, and given facilities not only for continuing in the standard of life of their parents, but also for improving this?

Such is the objection frequently urged. The right answer to it would seem to be that prudence is certainly always desirable, and that the Church by no means recommends parents to bring children into the world if and when there is no prospect of supporting them and bringing them up as children should be brought up. But it is only too easy to make this "Christian prudence" an excuse for very un-Christian selfishness and worldliness. Many parents enjoy in point of fact a standard of living which is far too high, and is by no

[1] *Encyclical on Christian Marriage*, C.T.S. edn., p. 8.
[2] *Ibid.*, p. 9.

means either necessary or desirable, particularly in the matter of pleasures. And moreover, children are far more likely to develop into satisfactory citizens of the State, and good members of God's Church, if they have had to carve their own careers by their own efforts, instead of being financed throughout by their parents, and placed in lucrative positions by them. It used to be urged that a man who has been educated at such and such a school must of course send his sons there, and the same applies to mothers and their daughters. And of course the income of the parents is such that it will permit of only one boy and/or only one girl being so educated! But if a choice has to be made between bringing into the world one or two such children, who are to be sent to the same expensive school as that attended by the parents themselves, or else to bring into the world more numerous children who must be sent to other and cheaper schools, which are not necessarily inferior in efficiency, then unhesitatingly the second course is to be recommended. In any case, there are such things as scholarships available for suitable children, and one of the best features of the recent Education Act is that it ensures more or less equal opportunities for all in the matter of education. Hence, this particular excuse for family limitation has now lost much of its force.

CHAPTER FOURTEEN

BIRTH CONTROL

THE subject of the size of the family, treated in the last chapter, naturally leads on to the subject of birth control. We can begin with a statement made by the late Father Bede Jarrett, O.P.:

> "Always ordinary traditional Christian teaching has allowed parents to space the arrival of their children; but it forbids this to be done by direct artificial interferences with nature. It recognises that the virtue of prudence, and also a variety of family necessities and difficulties may, under certain circumstances, allow a limitation to be set deliberately and legitimately to the number of children that parents may have. But it also considers that the will of man (plus the grace of God) is capable of carrying this out by the sole means of self-restraint. . . .
>
> "We cannot, indeed, but agree that economic conditions do now make the support of a large family harder than ever. But our answer to this problem is to urge as the remedy an increase of wages, and not a diminishing of the family. If one of these two things has to happen, let wages be altered, not the family."[1]

A certain spacing of children, then, is allowable, and even, in certain circumstances, but, we must add, not in all, some limitation of the number of children. But one thing is clear: this legitimate aim does not and cannot justify the use of means which are in themselves immoral and wrong. Now, inasmuch as the primary end of the marriage act is the procreation of children, it is necessarily immoral and wrong so to perform the act as deliberately to prevent it from fulfilling its natural purpose. As Pope Pius XI has put it:

> "Any use of matrimony whatsoever in the exercise of which the act is deprived, by human interference, of its natural power to procreate life, is an offence against the law of God and of nature, and those who commit it are guilty of a grave sin."[2]

From this we gather that, even from the standpoint of purely

[1] *The Catholic Mother*, with a Foreword by Cardinal Bourne, C.T.S., p. 5.
[2] *Encyclical on Christian Marriage*, C.T.S. edn. p. 26.

natural ethics, the use of artificial contraceptives is morally wrong. It is wrong precisely because it involves the full exercise of a natural function, and the satisfaction of a natural instinct, in such a way that the obvious natural aim and purpose of the function is frustrated. Such conduct is ethically a misuse of nature, a sin against nature, and therefore "unnatural", precisely in that sense.

Those who advocate or defend the use of contraceptives urge in reply that we are constantly acting in ways which are equally "un-natural", as when we shave, or amputate a limb and thus prevent it from fulfilling its natural function, and so on. Again, it is urged that the "story of civilisation itself has been the story of man's control over nature, mainly by mechanical means."[1]

In reply, we must point out that when we say birth control is "un-natural", we mean that it is against the natural *moral* law. Obviously, even contraceptives use natural laws and processes. But they use them in a way which is morally wrong. Equally, a man who murders another doubtless uses natural forces which he harnesses for the purpose, but that does not prevent his act from being morally wrong.

It is perfectly true that "civilisation has been the story of man's control over nature". But equally, as we realise especially to-day, it is possible to use this control over natural powers in an evil way and for evil ends.

As to shaving and such like acts which, it is urged, are equally "un-natural", we do not in these cases use a specifically natural function in such a way as to prevent it from attaining its natural end. We do not let the hair grow, and at the same time prevent this from achieving its normal end. Rather, we cut off the hair, and do our best to prevent its growth at all, and this we do because we consider we have a valid reason for so acting, and a reason which is ethically justifiable precisely because it is not using a function and at the same time depriving it of its natural end.

The matter will perhaps be clearer if we consider the case of the surgical operation, also urged in the objection. If it is necessary or desirable for the good of the organism as a whole, it is quite lawful and morally allowable to cut off a limb, and this precisely because *the parts of the body exist for the sake of the whole,* and thus, so far from acting against the "end" of the limb in question, we are in fact promoting it and ensuring its realisation. On the other hand, it cannot in any way be urged that the procreative function exists similarly only for the sake of the individual exercising it—this is not the case. Its primary purpose is the procreation of the race, and its

[1] Cf. *Report of National Council of Public Morals,* quoted by Fr. Henry Davis, S.J., in *Birth Control Ethics,* p. 17.

other purposes are only secondary to this. Now, artificial contraceptives are designed precisely to promote and allow the performance of the sex act in such a way as to frustrate its primary and natural purpose, and to replace this by a secondary end which thus becomes the primary and exclusive one, namely, the obtaining of the sex pleasure, etc. But that is essentially an overturning of the natural moral order, and no reasoning or excuse can make it right. Nor will it avail to urge that, in any case, the natural act is sometimes unable to produce its primary effect, by reason of some natural circumstances. In these cases, the obstacle is not one of human invention, or the result of deliberate human activity—it is precisely an obstacle due to nature itself, and therefore to Nature's God, who is the Sovereign Lord of Life and Death. There is a similar relation between these two things, the deliberate prevention of conception and the failure to conceive through natural defects, and between these two other things the deliberate killing of an innocent person, and his death by natural causes. *We* may not murder such a person, even though he will die naturally, and perhaps quite soon. Similarly *we* may not prevent conception, though God may will it not to take place.

The examples urged in the objection are not too happily chosen, and hardly provide exact parallels to the use of contraceptives. There is a much more suitable illustration. It has been brought forward by Dr. Halliday Sutherland, but advocates and defenders of contraceptives do not seem at all anxious to discuss it. The illustration consists in "what men did during the decline of the Roman Empire", in the matter of another natural function, namely, that of eating. As Dr. Halliday Sutherland says:

"They gorged themselves with the daintiest food *for the pleasure of eating*, and then, having visited the *vomitorium* (for it was all very scientifically arranged), they returned to the dinner-table, and commenced to eat again."[1]

The parallel to the use of contraceptives is fairly exact, for in each case we have the deliberate use of a natural function in such a way as to deprive it of its primary end. The primary end of eating is to nourish and feed the body, the secondary end is to satisfy our hunger and please the palate. The *vomitorium* provided the means of securing the secondary end of pleasing the palate, and at the same time frustrated the primary end. Thus, these people might well say: "We live to eat" instead of "we eat to live". In exactly the same way, the use of contraceptives exercises the sex function in such a way as to frustrate its natural and primary end, and allows only its

[1] *Birth Control Exposed*, p. 235.

secondary end, i.e., the satisfying of the appetite for sex pleasure.
Both these practices are morally wrong, and if one is to be defended
or advocated, so is the other. Yet advocates of birth control seem
strangely reluctant to come out into the open as champions of
gluttony and the *vomitorium*![1]

These considerations of natural reason are fortified by the teaching
of Revelation, studied and explained in Theology. Revelation, in
fact, contains a clear condemnation of one kind of birth control,
which obviously applies equally to modern artificial methods. This
condemnation goes back to the early days of the human race, as
these are narrated in the *Book of Genesis*. In ch. xxxviii we read that
Juda's first-born son took a wife named Thamar. But this son of
Juda was wicked in the sight of the Lord, and God slew him:

"Juda therefore said to Onan his (second) son: 'Go into thy
brother's wife, and marry her, that thou mayst raise seed to thy
brother. He, knowing that the children should not be his, when
he went in to his brother's wife, spilled his seed upon the ground,
lest children should be born in his brother's name. And therefore
the Lord slew him, because he did a detestable thing."[2]

This passage illustrates the "levirite law", set forth in *Deuteronomy*
xxv, 5-6:

"When brethren dwell together, and one of them dieth without
children, the wife of the deceased shall not marry to another, but
his brother shall take her, and raise up seed for his brother. And
the first son he shall have of her he shall call by his name, that his
name be not abolished out of Israel."[3]

Refusal to fulfil this law was punishable, not by death, be it noted,
but by an act publishing to all the dishonourable conduct of the
offender:

---

[1] The parallel between artificial contraceptives and the vomitorium is not *quite* exact,
as the act of contraception is one and the same as the performance of the sex act, whereas
the use of the vomitorium is a second act subsequent upon the first. Hence the un-
natural character of contraception is, so to speak, intrinsic and essential to the act,
whereas the vomitorium is an accidental supplement to the act of eating. This will
serve to explain why gluttony as such is only a venial sin, whereas the use of contraceptives is always mortal. In any case, as Father Henry Davis points out in his *Moral
and Pastoral Theology*, Vol. I, p. 244, gluttony "may accidentally be grievous in several
cases", one of which is "if it induces a man to find all his contentment in the gratifying
of his appetites". In such a case the sin is a mortal one, and this again is a circumstance
obviously present in the use of contraceptives.
[2] *Genesis* xxxviii, 8-10.
[3] *Deuteronomy* xxv 5-6.

"If he will not take his brother's wife, who by law belongeth to him, the woman shall go to the gate of the city, and call upon the ancients. . . . And they shall cause him to be sent for forthwith, and shall ask him. If he answer: 'I will not take her to wife,' the woman shall come to him before the ancients, and shall take off his shoe from his foot, and spit in his face, and say: 'So shall it be done to the man that will not build up his brother's house.' And his name shall be called in Israel, 'the house of the unshod.' "[1]

It is obvious, from a comparison of these passages of Scripture, that the slaying of Onan was not a punishment for his refusal to raise up seed to his brother—for that called for a much milder punishment—but it was inflicted upon him precisely because of his "detestable" act in his intercourse with Thamar.

Hence it is in vain that some modern non-Catholic exegetes and advocates of birth-control have tried to escape the force of this passage in *Genesis* by urging that Onan was punished merely for refusing to raise up seed to his brother, and that this constituted the "detestable act" referred to. Rather, as Dr. Skinner remarks in the volume on *Genesis* in the *International Critical Commentary*:

"Onan is slain because of the revolting manner in which he persistently evaded the sacred duty of raising up seed to his brother. It is not correct to say that his only offence was his selfish disregard of his deceased brother's interests."[2]

Thus is Catholic Tradition upheld by a modern non-Catholic scholar.

This interpretation of the sin of Onan is made absolutely certain for Catholics by the statement of Pope Pius XI in his *Encyclical on Christian Marriage*:

"We find evidence in the Sacred Scriptures that the Divine Majesty detests this unspeakable crime (the deliberate prevention of conception) with the deepest hatred, and has occasionally punished it with death, as St. Augustine observes: 'Sexual intercourse, even with a lawful wife, is unlawful and shameful if the conception of offspring is prevented. That is what Onan, the Son of Juda, did, and on that account God put him to death.' "[3]

If artificial contraceptives are thus excluded by reason and revelation, how is the spacing of births to be brought about, in cases

[1] *Deuteronomy* xxv, 7-10.
[2] *Genesis*, p. 454.
[3] C.T.S. edn., p. 25, but I have ventured to modify the translation on one point.

where such spacing is legitimate? There are two lawful and moral means. The first is complete abstention from the full marriage act when conception is not desired, and the second is the limitation of the sex act to times when conception is practically impossible, as expounded in the Ogino-Knaus theory.[1] We must point out that, in the opinion of many theologians, a good and sufficient moral reason is required for the limitation of intercourse to this "sterile period", and this harmonises with what we ourselves have said in an earlier chapter concerning the natural duty of married people to procreate children—and at least four if possible.

[1] For details, see Dr. Halliday Sutherland's *Laws of Life*, and *Control of Life*.

CHAPTER FIFTEEN

FAMILY LIFE AND PRAYERS

WE have now arrived at the stage in which we can contemplate the family in full being, with at least three, and preferably four or more children. It is to be hoped that these are living a true family life with their parents in their own home, and that, though education and recreation may take them outside it for a time, it still is regarded by them emphatically as their home. The family is the natural unit of society, which historically preceded the State, and it has its own inalienable rights and privileges. These it must jealously defend. Unfortunately, there has been a marked decay of family life in modern times, and a growth of irresponsible individualism. This trend should be checked, or else Society will inevitably suffer.

One feature used to characterise Christian homes, and that was the practice of family prayers. Unfortunately, this seems to be very rare nowadays. But a start should be made to revive it, by enthroning the Sacred Heart in the Home, and making this picture a centre of devotions, daily if possible, but if not at least weekly. The devotions should be those of the family as such, and all its members should be present, and if possible take part in it. Nothing is more calculated to bring home to all concerned the fact that the family is indeed a unit and a divinely instituted society, and not merely a collection of independent individuals.

This family spirit should be carried further still, and manifest itself in the corporate reception of Holy Communion in Church. This matter is one which presents certain difficulties. Most children attend a school, and in many places there are "School Communions" in Church, when the children are expected to sit with their fellow scholars and receive Holy Communion with them. This practice doubtless has its advantages, but it also has disadvantages, and it should always be remembered that the child belongs primarily to his parents and his family, and only secondarily to the school. The teacher, after all, occupies his position only because he stands *in loco parentis*. The present writer has heard of a case in which a teacher in a Catholic elementary school tried to insist that one particular child should sit and receive with the other children, and *not* with his own parents. The parish priest in this case was a strong-minded man, who knew what was right and fitting, and he decided that the child should sit and receive Communion with his parents. But he had to encounter and overcome very strong opposition on the part of the teacher in question.

In connection with the subject of family prayers, we wish to call attention to some very beautiful prayers which the Church has set forth for the use of parents and their children, and to which she has attached indulgences. Here, in the first place, is a prayer to the Sacred Heart of Jesus, to be said by husband and wife:

"O most sacred Heart of Jesus, King and Centre of all hearts, take up thy dwelling and reign in our hearts, and through thy grace make us to love each other chastely and truly, as Thou didst love thy immaculate spouse the Church, and didst give thyself for her.

"Grant to us that mutual charity and Christian indulgence which is so highly acceptable to thee, and a mutual patience in tolerating faults; for we know that no creature is lacking in these. Do not allow even the slightest injury to that sweet harmony of minds which is the basis of that mutual help in the many and varied necessities of life, for it was to this end that woman was created and inseparably joined to her husband.

"Cause to reign amongst us, O Lord God, a perpetual and holy endeavour to live a truly Christian life, so that the image of thine own mystical marriage with thy Holy Church may ever shine forth more and more, which image thou didst deign to impress upon us in the happy day of our union. Grant, we beseech thee, that the good example of our own lives may help our children, and be a powerful stimulus to leading lives in harmony with thy holy law; and finally, after this our exile, may we ascend to heaven where, with the help of thy grace, which we earnestly beg, we shall remain with them for ever, and deserve to praise and bless thee for ever. Amen."

To this prayer is attached an indulgence of three hundred days.[1]

Next, here is a prayer which parents can recite for their children:

"O Lord God, who in calling us to matrimony, hast deigned to make us fruitful, and dost give to this sublime state in which we have been placed by thee, the joy of being a certain image of thine own infinite fecundity, we ardently commend to thee our most beloved children. We place them in thy paternal charge and almighty patronage, that they may ever grow together in thy holy

[1] Sacred Penitentiary, 11th Dec. 1923 and 25th Nov. 1936; *Preces et Pia Opera*, no. 706.

fear, live a thoroughly Christian life, and be a solace not only to us, who have given them life, but especially to thee, their Creator.

"Behold, O Lord, the ways of those around us: behold the cunning manner in which men everywhere try to corrupt others by false doctrines and evil examples. Watch over our children, to help and defend them, O Lord, and grant that they may be preserved from these great dangers and that, by the right example of our own lives and morals, and the perfect observance of thy holy law and those of Holy Mother Church, we may be able to lead them in the paths of virtue and of thy commandments. But all our labour will be in vain unless thou, O almighty and merciful God, make it fruitful with thy heavenly benediction.

"We therefore beg from thee this blessing from the bottom of our hearts, and trusting in thy great goodness and mercy, bestowed upon us both for ourselves and for those children thou hast willed to give us. To thee, O Lord, we consecrate them; keep them as the apple of thine eye, protect them under the shadow of thy wings, and grant that, together with them, we may be able to reach heaven, giving thanks for the care which thou hast had of our whole family, O loving Father, and that we may praise thee for ever. Amen."

To this prayer an indulgence of three hundred days is likewise attached.[1]

---

[1] Sacred Penitentiary, 25th Nov. 1836; *Preces et Pia Opera*, no. 707.

CHAPTER SIXTEEN

THE SEX INSTRUCTION OF CHILDREN

WE now come to the difficult and delicate question of the instruction of children on matters of sex. There has been much opposition on the part of some Catholics to any instruction of children in such things, and many have held that such instruction should never be given at all. Apparently they were quite willing that their children should discover the "facts of life", either through unsavoury sources, or by their own personal and sad experience. It is hardly possible to imagine a graver neglect of parental duty. And hardly less grave must be the responsibility of those parents who deliberately tell lies to their children when these innocently ask questions on the subject. Sooner or later the child will realise that the parents have lied in the matter, and the shock to respect for parents is and must be very great indeed.

Fortunately, in this matter of sex instruction, we now have very clear guidance given us by our Catholic authorities. The Church insists that the careful training of the will is far more important than the mere imparting of knowledge in this matter, and certainly a moment's reflection must serve to show that mere instruction in the details and mysteries of sex and the procreation of children might well constitute a great source of temptation, inflame the passions, and arouse sex desires, and thus become a serious occasion of sin.

Accordingly, the Church authorities are opposed to ordinary secular and public instruction in sex matters by teachers in schools. She prefers that such instruction as is necessary or desirable should be given privately, by parents in the first place, or else by those whose duty and privilege it is to train the young. There are no less than three recent Papal documents bearing on this matter.

The first is a passage in the Encyclical of Pope Pius XI on the Christian Education of Youth. Here the Pope warns Catholics against that "very grave danger" constituted by the fact that "naturalism is nowadays invading the field of education in a most delicate matter of purity of morals." The Pope develops the subject thus:

"Far too common is the error of those who, with dangerous assurance and under an ugly term, propagate a so-called sex-

education, falsely imagining they can forearm youths against the
dangers of sensuality by means purely natural, such as a foolhardy
initiation and precautionary instruction for all indiscriminately,
even in public; and, worse still, by exposing them at an early age
to the occasions, in order to accustom them, so it is argued, and
as it were to harden them against such dangers.

"Such persons grievously err in refusing to recognise the
inborn weakness of human nature, and the law of which the
Apostle speaks, fighting against the law of the mind; and also in
ignoring the experience of facts, from which it is clear that,
particularly in young people, evil practices are the effect, not so
much of ignorance of intellect as of weakness of a will exposed to
dangerous occasions and unsupported by the means of grace."[1]

Then the Pope points out the opportuneness of private instruction
on such matters:

"In this extremely delicate matter, if, all things considered,
some private instruction is found necessary and opportune, from
those who hold from God the commission to teach and who have
the grace of their state, every precaution must be taken. . . .
'Speaking generally, during the period of childhood it suffices to
employ those remedies which produce the double effect of open-
ing the door to the virtue of chastity and closing the door upon
vice.' "[2]

The Encyclical upon Christian Education was issued in 1929.
Two years later, i.e., in March 1931, the Holy Office published an
answer to the question: "Is the method known as Sexual Education
or Initiation to be approved?" The reply was as follows:

"This method cannot be approved. On the contrary, the faithful should train the young by using that method employed up to
the present time by the Church. . . . Their first care must be to
give the youth of both sexes a strong, thorough and uninterrupted
instruction in their religion; teaching them to esteem, love and
desire the angelic virtue,[3] urging them to have recourse to prayer

---

[1] On the Christian Education of Youth. C.T.S. edn., p. 31.
[2] Ibid., pp. 31-32. The Pope is here quoting from an Italian work on education by
Antoniano. The C.T.S. translation speaks of the "virtue of purity". But the original
has "castità", and I have modified the translation accordingly. There is no such thing
as a separate "virtue of purity", as I have pointed out in an earlier chapter (see Part Two,
pp. 116-117).
[3] In his C.T.S. pamphlet, Training in Purity, Canon Mahoney translates this phrase
thus: "teaching them to esteem and love the angelic virtue of purity." This suffers
from a two-fold defect. First it omits to translate "desiderium", and secondly, it
speaks of the "virtue of purity" where the original speaks of the "angelic virtue".

and the sacraments of Penance and the Holy Eucharist, fostering
in them a filial devotion to Our Blessed Lady, the Mother of
holy purity, under whose protection they should place themselves
without reserve; teaching them carefully to avoid dangerous
books, obscene spectacles, unclean conversations, and every
other occasion of sin. . . ."[1]

Lastly, on October 26th, 1941, Pope Pius XII gave an important
Address to Catholic Mothers, containing explicit and definite advice
as to how parents should instruct their children in sex matters:

"You will not fail to watch for and to discern the moment in
which certain unspoken questions have occurred to the minds of
your children, and are troubling their senses. It will then be your
duty to your daughters, the father's duty to your sons, carefully
and delicately to unveil the truth so far as it appears necessary, to
give a prudent, true and Christian answer to these questions, and
set their minds at rest. If imparted by the lips of Christian parents,
at the proper time, in the proper measure, and with the proper
precautions, the revelation of the mysterious and marvellous laws
of life will be received by them with reverence and gratitude, and
will enlighten their minds with far less danger than if they
learned them haphazard, from some unpleasant shock, from secret
conversations, through over-sophisticated companions, or from
clandestine reading, the more dangerous and pernicious as secrecy
inflames the imagination and troubles the senses. Your words, if
they are wise and discreet, will prove a safeguard and a warning
in the midst of the temptations and the corruptions which sur-
round them."[2]

To these Papal pronouncements we must add the important Joint
Pastoral Letter issued by the Catholic Archbishops and Bishops of
England and Wales entitled *The Catholic Attitude to Sex Education,*
in which the matter is further explained and developed. The
bishops emphasise that, in the matter of sex education, "teachers
have no strict right to arrogate to themselves parental duties; if
called upon by the parents to deputise for them in this delicate
matter, they may very properly do so", but such instruction on "the

True, the Holy Office goes on to speak of Our Lady as the "Mother of holy purity".
Equally, the Litany of Our Lady calls her "Mater purissima". But that does not signify
that there is such a thing as a "virtue of purity", as distinct from the traditional "virtue
of chastity". Cf. Part Two, pp. 116–117.

[1] Cf. Canon Mahoney's *Training in Purity,* pp. 3-4. The Latin text of the Decree will
be found in the *Clergy Review,* June 1931, p. 637.

[2] Mahoney, *op. cit.,* p. 4; the whole address is published by the C.T.S. under the title
The Pope Speaks to Mothers.

more intimate matters of life must always remain personal and individual. Class or group instruction of children or of youth on the physiological aspect of sex would be fraught with grave dangers, and would be against the traditional teaching of the Church."[1]

It is important to note that, in any case, the Church does not encourage either parents or teachers to give wrong answers to children's questions on sex. The English bishops here quote the Address of Pope Pius XII to Catholic Mothers once more:

> "Train the mind of your children; do not give them wrong ideas or wrong reasons for things; whatever their questions may be, do not answer them with evasions or untrue statements which their minds rarely accept, but take occasion from them lovingly and paternally to train their minds, which want only to open to the truth and to grasp it with the first ingenuous gropings of their reasoning and reflective powers."[2]

While giving full weight to the Papal and episcopal condemnation of public and general instruction on the intimate details of sex, we must not infer that all instruction on sex in schools is forbidden or discouraged by the Church. On the contrary, the preceding chapters of this book will have shown that a full and comprehensive knowledge of the Church's general teaching is impossible without some knowledge of sex. Sex occurs in the teaching concerning the Creation, and the Fall; Sex also, as we have seen, occupies a definite place in the Church's teaching on the Virginity of Mary, the Incarnation, the Sacrament of Matrimony, the Virginal life and celibacy, etc. It would not be possible, then, to exclude sex altogether from the curriculum of Catholic schools, nor is it in any way desirable that this should be done. But the teaching should be general, and should certainly *not* descend to unnecessary physiological details concerning the process of reproduction, at least in the human species.

We say "at least in the human species", for in schools where biology and natural history are taught—and it is in every way desirable that these should form part of the curriculum in every modern Catholic school—the subject of reproduction will necessarily and naturally occur. Here the teacher—and also the parent— will find a method of imparting to the child much *indirect* knowledge concerning the process of sexual generation, which will provide the basis for such further private instruction concerning human reproduction as and when this is thought necessary or desirable. The child's mind will in the meantime have become accustomed to the

[1] C.T.S. edn., p. 4.
[2] C.T.S. edn., p. 9.

idea of the differentiation of the sexes, and of sex organs, by a study of plant and animal life, and will realise that a union of the sexual gametes—or "fertilisation"—is necessary for the production of a new individual in the higher species. Further, the germination of a seed in the ground, or the growth of an embryonic animal either in its mother's body or in a fertilised ovum or egg deposited outside, will prepare the child for the time when it is desirable to acquaint him or her with the wonderful and glorious power of reproduction possessed also by human beings. Taken in conjunction with the religious teaching on the Creation of Man, the Virtue of Chastity, and the Sacrament of Marriage, such biological instruction will prepare the child's mind quite naturally for the imparting privately of further knowledge concerning sex and marriage, when the time comes for this to be done. This new teaching will be fitted into its proper place in the child's mind, and will naturally be grafted on to the general conception of sex already present there, and the result will be a sound, healthy, and truly Catholic attitude on this matter.

Obviously there will never be any need to insinuate, much less to teach openly, that sexual matters are in any way "dirty" or "impure". We must always insist and instil into the child that what is impure is, not the use of sex, but its abuse or misuse. We must accordingly be very careful how we inculcate true modesty. But that subject has already been dealt with in a special chapter in the Second Part.

And thus I bring to an end this lengthy consideration of the Mystery of Sex. I dedicated it in the beginning to my parents, who, under God, gave me my being. To whom should I entrust it, in the end, but to the Blessed Virgin Mary, the Second Eve, who is the Mother of all the living in the order of grace, as the first Eve was in the order of Nature, and who is not only the Virginal Mother of the Word Incarnate, but also of all his brethren.

Mater castissima, ora pro nobis.

APPENDIX

SELECT BIBLIOGRAPHY

BIOLOGY, ETC.

Fundamentals of Biology, by J. W. Stork, M.A. and L. P. W. Renouf, B.A. John Murray, 1935.

Principles of Biology, by G. Waddington, S.J., Ph.D., in collaboration with Monica Taylor, S.N.D., D.Sc. John Murray, 1935.

Education and Biology, by J. A. Lauwerys, Bs.C. Sands, 1934.

Physiology of Sex, by Kenneth Walker, M.D. Pelican Books, 1941.

Encyclopædia of Sex Practice. Torch Publishing Co.

GENERAL.

The Catholic Doctor, by Rev. A. Bonnar, O.F.M., D.D. Burns Oates, 1943.

Body and Spirit: Essays in Sexuality, by various writers. Translated by Donald Attwater. Longmans, 1939.

Mental Deficiency, its Causes, Prevention and Cure, by M. MacGown, M.B., Ch.B. Catholic Truth Society.

State Sterilisation of the Unfit, by Rev. Henry Davis, S.J. Burns Oates, 1931.

The Case against Sterilisation, by Dr. L. Fairfield. C.T.S.

Catholic Teaching on Abortion, by Rev. Henry Davis, S.J. C.T.S.

Outline of Psychiatry, by John D. O'Brien, M.D., B.S. Herder, 1934.

Modesty, by J. de la Vaissiere, S.J. Translated by S. A. Raemers, Ph.D. Herder, 1937.

Retours en Chrétienté: La Naissance, Le Mariage, La Mort, by Pierre Doncoeur. Paris: Grasset, 1933.

Pastoral. Medicine, by Rev. L. Ruland, D.D., Professor of Moral and Pastoral Theology in the University of Wurzburg. Adapted into English by Rev. T. A. Rattler, O.S.A. Herder, 1934.

A Great Mystery of Inheritance, by Constance M. Symonds. Burns Oates, 1925.

Morals and Marriage: The Catholic Background to Sex, by T. G. Wayne. Longmans, 1936.

MARRIAGE.

To Those Getting Married, by W. Jewell. C.T.S.

Training for Marriage, by Rev. A. Gits, S.J. C.T.S.

Wedlock, by Rev. C. C. Martindale, S.J. Sheed & Ward, 1937.

Marrying a Catholic, by Mgr. P. Hallett. C.T.S.

Holiness of Married Life, by Archbishop Godfrey. C.T.S.

Duties of Married Life, by Cardinal Mercier. C.T.S.

Marriage: the Christian Ideal, by Mrs. Wilfrid Ward. C.T.S.

I'm Keeping Company, by Rev. F. Meyer, O.F.M. Cincinnati, St. Francis Bookshop, 1934.
Love, Marriage and Chastity, by Rev. E. Mersch, S.J. Sheed & Ward, 1939.
Marriage and Parenthood, the Catholic Ideal, by Rev. T. J. Gerrard, New York: Wagner, 1937.
Conception Chrétienne de la Famille, by J. Terrel. Brussels, Etudes Religieuses.
Morale Familiale, by P. Mélin. Bloud & Gay.

PARENTS AND CHILDREN.
Duties of Parents towards their Children, by B. Wolferstan, S.J. C.T.S.
The Catholic Mother, by Rev. Bede Jarrett, with Introduction by Cardinal Bourne. C.T.S.
The Expectant Mother, by Mrs. Blundell. C.T.S.
Preparing our Daughters for Life, by a Catholic Mother. C.T.S.
The Daughters of To-day, by Mrs. Blundell. C.T.S.
Mothers in Wartime, by Mrs. Blundell. C.T.S.
The Unmarried Mother and her Child, by Mary Cunnane, S.R.N. C.T.S.
Women's Duties in Social and Political Life, by Pope Pius XII. C.T.S.
The Pope Speaks to Mothers. C.T.S.

MARRIAGE AND DIVORCE.
Christian Marriage, by Pope Pius XI. C.T.S.
Divorce, by W. Jewell. C.T.S.
Divorce in the New Testament, by R. E. Hall, M.A. C.T.S.
Why we Resist Divorce, by Rev. H. Thurston, S.J. C.T.S.
Marriage and Divorce, by Rev. J. Kendal, O.S.B. C.T.S.

BIRTH CONTROL.
Towards Moral Bankruptcy, by Paul Bureau. With Introduction by Dr. Mary Scharlieb. Sands, 1925.
Birth Control: Ethical, Social and Moral Objections, by Dr. Halliday Sutherland. C.T.S.
The Great Refusal, by G. Whitworth. London, F. Muller Ltd., 1942.
The Unborn Millions, by Norman Maclean, D.D. C.T.S.
A City Full of Boys and Girls, by a Catholic Woman Doctor. C.T.S.
A Talk to Catholic Wives, by a Catholic Woman Doctor. C.T.S.
The Declining Birth Rate, by Rev. H. Thurston, S.J. C.T.S.
Birth Control: Medical and Ethical Aspects, by a Doctor and a Priest. C.T.S.
Thou Shalt not Kill: A Brief for the Unborn Child, by Dr. George Clement. Philadelphia: Peter Reilly Co., 1936.
Judgment on Birth Control, by R. de Guchteneere, M.A. Sheed & Ward, 1943.
Birth Control: The Fallacies of Dr. M. Stopes, by Rev. Henry Davis, S.J. Burns Oates, 1928.
Birth Control Ethics, by the same. Burns Oates, 1926.
Contraception and Psychology, by Rev. C. C. Martindale, S.J. League of National Life.

The Moral Argument against Birth Control, by the Rev. T. E. Flynn. *Dublin Review.*

Ethics of Birth Control: Report of the Special Committee appointed by the National Council of Public Morals. Macmillan, 1925.

Mariage et Natalité, Congres de la Natalite. Brussels, 1934.

Marriage and Periodic Abstinence, by J. G. Holt, M.D. Longmans, 1938.

The Rhythm, by L. Latz, M.D. Illinois Latz Foundation, 1932.

The Case against Birth Control, by E. Roberts Moore, Ph.D. New York Century Co., 1931.

Birth Control Exposed, by Dr. Halliday Sutherland. Cecil Palmer, 1925.

Laws of Life, by the same. Sheed & Ward, 1935.

Control of Life, by the same. Burns Oates, 1944.

The Night Hoers, or the Case against Birth Control, by A. M. Ludovici. Herbert Jenkins, 1928.

SEX EDUCATION.

Sex Teaching in Schools, National Union of Teachers, 1944.

Sex Instruction, by P. J. Bruckner, S.J. St. Louis, 1937.

Catholic Attitude to Sex Education: Joint Pastoral Letter of the Catholic Bishops of England and Wales. C.T.S., 1944.

For Boys and Men, by Rev. J. M. McGovern. C.T.S.

Preparing for Manhood, by Rev. A. Chapple. C.T.S.

What is Purity? by Rev. T. Corbishley, S.J. Manresa Press.

Training in Purity, by Very Rev. Canon Mahoney. C.T.S.

The Sex Education of Children: A Simple Guide for Parents, by a Catholic Woman Doctor, C.T.S.

Peter and Veronica, by Margaret Beech. Herbert Jenkins, 1928.

Peter and Veronica Growing Up, by the same. Herbert Jenkins, 1935.

The Difficult Commandment, by Rev. C. C. Martindale, S.J. Manresa Press.

Into their Company, by a Medical Woman, a Girl and a Wife, with Introduction by Rev. C. C. Martindale, S.J. Burns Oates, 1930.

Growing Up; A Book for Girls.

Sex Enlightenment and the Catholic, by Rev. J. Leycester King, S.J. Bellarmine Series, Burns Oates.

Sex Instruction, by James J. Walsh, M.D., Ph.D. New York: Wagner, 1931.

L'Education de la Chasteté, by A. Knoch, Docteur en Theologie, Chanoine Honoraire de la Cathédrale de Liége, 4th edn., 1921.

THEOLOGY OF SEX AND MARRIAGE.

Some works have been mentioned under other sections. The standard works and sources are mentioned throughout the present work.

INDEX

Antoniano, 62
Aquinas, St. Thomas, on woman as help-
    mate for man, 10
— on virginity and its social aspect,
    13–15
— evangelical counsels not for all, 15
— on sex act as hindrance to contem-
    plation, 32
— on sex act as act of virtue of justice, 33
— on sex act as act of virtue of religion,
    33
— on social aspect of marriage and vir-
    ginity, 13, 14, 49
Ambrose, St., on nuptial veil, 23
Augustine, St., on woman as helpmate for
    man, 10
— on abstention from marriage act, 48
— on onanism, 56

Beales, A. C. F., 49
Bedchamber, bridal, blessing of, 26
Bees and neuters, 11
Biology and sex instruction, 64
Birth control, 52–57
— doctors and, 5, 6
— and contraceptives, 30
Breasts, blessing of, 42
Brittany, abstinence from sex act in, 35
Browning, Robert, on sex union, 28
Burton, Doris, 43

Canon Law and engagements, 20
Canons of Hippolytus, 44
Chastity and sex instruction, 65
Childbirth, Church and, 44–47
— intercourse before and after, 36–38
— ritual stain of, 45
— possibility of sin in, 45
— physical consequences of, 45
Children, sex characteristics of, 8
— education of, 9
— sex instruction of, 61–65
Clergy Review, 25
Concupiscence, 39
Co-education, 9
Communion, Holy, and Sex Act, 24, 32
Contemplation and virginity, 13–14
Contraceptives. See Birth Control
Corinthians, I, 24, 33, 48
Counsels, evangelical, not for all, 15
Creation, doctrine on, and sex instruction,
    64, 65
Crew, Prof. F. A. E., 4, 5

Davis, Rev. H., S.J., 33, 53, 55
Defectives, marriage of, 16, 17
Deuteronomy, 55, 56
Dictionnaire Apologétique, 24
Doctors and birth control, 5, 6
Doncoeur, P., 22, 23
Droit du Seigneur, 24

Education Act, 51
Education and sex, 29. Cf. Children, in-
    struction of
Ellis, Havelock, 6
Embryo, growth of, 3
Encyclopædia of Sex, 36, 37
Engagements, 20
Ephesians, Epistle to, 32
Eschbach, 36
Eugenics and Eugenists, 16

Fall, doctrine of, and sex instruction, 64
Fallon, Père, S.J., 17
Family a natural society, 10, 58
— size of, 48–51, 57, 58
— prayers, 58–60
— Communions, 58, 59
Fertilisation of ovum by spermatozoon,
    3, 4, 65
Finis operis, 6
Finis operantis, 6
Fœtus, 37
Fortescue, 25
Frigidity, 30

Gametes, male and female, 3, 6, 7, 65
Genesis, 10, 48, 55
Gousset, Cardinal, 48, 49
Gray, Dr. A. Charles, 6

Holy Office and Sex Instruction, 62, 63
Husbands and wives, 27
— complementary to each other, 9
Hymen, 28

Incarnation and sex instruction, 64
Innocence, State of, virginity and mother-
    hood combined in, 1, 15
Inhibitions and sex act, 29
Instinct and reason, 10
Intercourse, see Sex Act
International Critical Commentary, 56

Jarrett, Fr. Bede, O.P., 52

Joint Pastoral of English Bishops on Sex Education, 63, 64
Joseph, St., abstinence from sex act in honour of, 35

King, Sir F. Truby, 37
King, Mary Truby, 37
Kiss in Nuptial Mass, 23
Kiss in marriage, 30

Levirite law, 55, 56
Leviticus, 36
Lies not to be told to children in sex matters, 64
Litany of Loretto, 65
Love on the Dole, 17
— and marriage, 18, 19, 27
Lust, 27

Mace, Dr. David, on sexual intimacy, 5
— says sex union outside marriage is only a mistake, 6
Mahoney, Canon, 25, 62, 63
Marriage, contract of, 29
— how and why natural, 7
— raised to a sacrament by Christ, 1, 11, 16, 65
— received in mortal sin, 24
— and sex instruction, 64
— State and, 11
— precept concerning, 15, 48–50, 57
— right to, 16
— of defectives, 16, 17
— social aspect of, 17, 18, 49
— and economic considerations, 17, 52
— prudence in, 17, 18, 50, 52
— choice of partner, 18, 19
— love in, 18, 19
— attacks on, 19
— exchange of medical certificates, 19
— ceremonies of, 21–26
— mixed, 21
Martindale, Rev. Fr., on Churching of Women, 45
Mass, Nuptial, 21, 24
— kiss in, 23
— exhortation in, 23, 24
Mary, B. V., 45–47
— abstinence from sex act in honour of, 35
— Purification of, 44
— Virginity of, and Sex instruction, 64
— Second Eve, 65
Medical certificates and marriage, 19
Méline, P., 48, 49
Menopause, intercourse during and after, 38, 39
Menstruation, 8, 36
Miscarriage can be caused by intercourse during pregnancy, 37

Modesty, 65
Mothercraft system, 37

National Council of Public Morals, Report of, 53
Newsom, G. E., 4
Nuptial Blessing, 22–25
Nuptial Mass, 21, 24
Nuptial veil, 23

O'Connell, 25
Ogino-Knaus theory, 57
O'Kane, 24, 25, 44
Onan, sin of, 55, 56
Ordo Administrandi, 25
Outline of Modern Knowledge, 4
Ovary, 3
Ovum, 3, 4, 6, 8, 37, 65

Parents and marriage of children, 19, 20
Paul, St., and abstinence from sex act, 24, 36
— on duties of husbands and wives, 27
— on doing all things for God's glory, 32
— on our union with Christ, 32
— on use of marriage act, 48
Pius X on sex act and Holy Communion, 24
Pius XI on right to marry, 16, 17
— on choice of a partner, 18, 19
— on love, 27
— on religious character of sex act, 31
— on primary and secondary ends of sex act, 39
— on blessing of offspring, 50
— on wrongful use of marriage act, 52, 56
— on sex instruction, 61, 62
Pius XII on sex instruction, 63, 64
Pope, Fr. Hugh, O.P., 33
Preces et Pia Opera, 59, 60
Pregnancy, intercourse during, 36–38
— religious aspect of, 40–43
Psalm xxiii, 45
— lxvi, 41
— cxxvii, 25
Puberty, age of, 8
Purification of B.V.M., 44
Purification of Women after childbirth, 44
Purity, 14, 65

Reproduction, asexual, 5
— sexual, 3–7, 64, 65
— is the biological purpose of the sex act, 3–5
Right to marry, 16
Rituale Romanum and Nuptial Mass, 24
— and blessing of nuptial bedchamber, 26
— and blessing of pregnant woman, 40–42
— and blessing of children, 44

Ruland, Rev. Dr., 37, 38

Sacred Heart, prayer to, 59
Safe period, 39
Sarum rite, 44
— blessing of bedchamber in, 26
Schools, sex instruction in, 64
Self preservation, instinct of, 15
Secondary sex characteristics, 8
Sex in natural science, 3–7
— not a concession but a holy insti-
    tution, 1
— social aspect of, 10–15
Sex act, lawfulness for various ends, 2, 6,
    39, 52
— as expression of mutual love, 27–30, 39
— abstinence from, 2, 24, 32, 34, 35
— biological purpose is reproduction,
    3–5
— symbolises spiritual union, 27, 28
— symbolises union between Christ and
    the Church, 28, 32
— difficulties in performance of, 28, 29
— and inhibitions, 29
— should be preceded by acts of court-
    ship, 29
— morality of subsidiary acts, 30
— religious character of, 31–33
— and Holy Communion, 24, 32
— and sin, 32, 33
— frequency of, 35, 36
— as act of justice, 33, 35
— during menstrual period, 36
— during pregnancy, 36–38
— after childbirth, 38, 39
— during and after change of life, 38, 39
— and contraceptives, etc., 52–54
Sex instinct a social one, 11
Sex instruction of children, 61–65
Sex organs, 65
Sex pleasure and reproduction, 5
Sexual pessimism, 1
School Communions, 58
Skinner, Dr., 56

Spermatozoon, 3, 6, 65
State and marriage, 11
— power of, 38
— and family, 58
State in life, choice of, 16
Sterilisation, 5
Sterility, 6
— prayers in case of, 46, 47
Student Christian Movement, 5
Sutherland, Dr. Halliday, on Safe Period,
    39, 57
— on Vomitorium, 54, 55

Taparelli, 49
Tobias, 24, 34, 35
Trobriand Islanders, 4, 6

Vermeersch, 33
Virginity, superiority of, over marriage,
    if fruitful, 1, 2
— praiseworthy only in present state of
    mankind, 1
— not laudable in state of innocence, 15
— natural basis of, 12
— is essentially social, 12
— St. Thomas on, 12–15
— and contemplation, 12–14
— not for all, 15, 16
— and sex instruction, 64
Virginity of B.V.M. praiseworthy be-
    cause fruitful, 2
Vomitorium, 54, 55

Walker, Mr. Kennet, on variations in
    sexuality, 11
— on continence, 11, 12
— on medical certificates before mar-
    riage, 19, 20
— on frigidity, etc., 29, 30
Weatherhead, Rev. L., 5
Wedding ring, indulgence for kissing, 21,
    22
Wife a helpmate of husband, 10
Woman, characteristics of, 9, 10